Fundamentals
of Mariology

FUNDAMENTALS
of MARIOLOGY

BY

JUNIPER B. CAROL, O.F.M.

BENZIGER BROTHERS, Inc.
NEW YORK
BOSTON, CINCINNATI, CHICAGO, SAN FRANCISCO

Imprimi potest:

CELSUS WHEELER, O.F.M.
Provincial

Nihil obstat:

JOHN A. GOODWINE, J.C.D.
Censor Librorum

Imprimatur:

✠FRANCIS CARDINAL SPELLMAN
Archbishop of New York

New York   March 23, 1956

The Nihil obstat and Imprimatur are official declarations that a book is free from doctrinal or moral error. No implication is contained therein that those who have granted the Nihil obstat and Imprimatur agree with the contents, opinions, or statements expressed

To His Eminence

Emmanuel Cardinal Arteaga y Betancourt

Archbishop of Havana

As a token

of my profound gratitude

and veneration

The Author

PREFATORY NOTE

ONE of the most striking phases of Catholic life in the United States is the growing desire of the younger laity for instruction in the science of theology, particularly on the college level. This desire is matched by the zeal of educators in Catholic colleges and universities to provide adequate courses in the sacred sciences. A convincing witness of the health of the movement is the Society of Catholic College Teachers of Sacred Doctrine. Although the organization was founded only a few years ago, it has achieved astounding success, and is unremitting in its efforts to improve the quality of theological instruction by clarifying objectives, devising programs, and establishing ideals for teacher training.

Yet a distressing obstacle encountered in all endeavors to teach sacred doctrine in a satisfactory way is the woeful dearth of good textbooks in English. A few series of texts have been written in recent years but have not gained wide acceptance. This is true of theology in general, and is especially applicable to that part of theology which is Mariology. Some books, which were highly esteemed in their day, are by now antiquated, such as the Pohle-Preuss *Mariology*. Others, like *The Mother of the Savior and Our Interior Life* by Garrigou-Lagrange or the two-volume *Mariology* by Scheeben, are quite unsuited for classroom use. Accordingly teachers of Mariology in colleges and universities, as well as professors of theology in seminaries, will welcome the appearance of *Fundamentals of Mariology* by the learned theologian, Father Juniper B. Carol, O.F.M.

The author was admirably equipped to undertake his task. He is unquestionably the most prominent Mariologist in the United States and ranks with the best in the world. His scores of articles on various aspects of his favorite subject have appeared in many journals in Europe and America. The greatest of his books thus far published is his monumental volume, *De Corredemptione Beatae Virginis Mariae*, which has won universal acclaim. The indefatigable Franciscan is the founder of the Mariological Society of America and is the editor of its annual proceedings, *Marian Studies*. At the present time he is directing the most ambitious Mariological project ever undertaken in our country, the three-volume set entitled *Mariology*, to which he has also contributed several papers. *Fundamentals of Mariology* has no counterpart in the English language. It is the fruit of ripened scholarship and, no less pertinently, reveals the experience of years spent in teaching Mariology.

Rev. Cyril Vollert, S.J., President,
The Mariological Society of America

St. Marys, Kansas
September 25, 1955.

Introduction

THE present book aims to satisfy the repeated requests addressed to the author from various quarters, urging him to publish the series of Mariology lectures which he offers regularly at St. Bonaventure University. The lectures, given since 1952 and only during the summer course, have been attended normally by graduate students of the Department of Sacred Sciences, mostly sisters, and a few priests and seminarians. The publication of these lectures in book-form is intended to serve primarily as a textbook for seminaries and similar institutions for religious, although it is likewise suitable for instructing the laity, and even for supplying a theological basis to our Marian preaching.

It is common knowledge that in years gone by, the teaching of Mariology in most seminaries was reduced to a few sketchy lessons on the more important theses of the tract, such as the divine Maternity, the Immaculate Conception, and the Assumption. The reason invariably given by the theology professor was that the already overcrowded curriculum hardly allowed time for expanding on this secondary treatise. The situation was being deplored already at the close of the sixteenth century when Suárez rightly complained that theologians devoted endless *disputationes* to discuss the nature and attributes of

the angels, while they allotted comparatively little space
to the treatment of God's Mother, the Queen of Angels.

Fortunately, these lamentable conditions have im-
proved considerably in more recent times. The day has
finally come when Mariology is being accorded its right-
ful place within the theological system, and is beginning
to receive the attention it deserves in the seminary classroom. No doubt, the repeated Marian pronouncements
of recent popes have contributed much to correct the
unreasonable disproportion alluded to, by stimulating a
deeper and broader appreciation of Our Blessed Lady's
unique prerogatives, particularly her prominent position
in the economy of our Redemption.

As the title of our book sufficiently indicates, these
are not fully developed discourses on Our Lady, but
rather briefly summarized lessons, some of them in almost outline form, on the various theses integrating the
entire corpus of Marian theology. It will be the task of
the teacher to enlarge on the more important questions
and, whenever the circumstances demand it, to explain
more fully certain technical expressions which may be
unfamiliar to the layman.

In harmony with our purpose in publishing these
notes, we have retained the language, style and manner
of presentation proper to a textbook. For the benefit of
those wishing to pursue further the study of particular
questions, representative and up-to-date bibliographical
references have been added in the footnotes. In the
general division and presentation of the matter, we have

followed, for the most part, the excellent *Mariologia* of Father Gabriel M. Roschini, O.S.M., although recourse to several other well-known authors has been frequent and profitable.

If these outlines should arouse in the reader even a tenuous desire to enrich his fund of knowledge concerning the sublime mission and unparalleled prerogatives of Our Immaculate Mother, the author's labors would be amply rewarded.

CONTENTS

Part One

THE SINGULAR MISSION OF MARY

Part Two

THE SINGULAR PREROGATIVES OF MARY

SECTION ONE

Prerogatives Conferred on Mary at the Beginning of Her Life

SECTION TWO

*Prerogatives Conferred on Mary During
the Course of Her Life*

SECTION THREE

Prerogatives Conferred on Mary
at the End of Her Life

Abbreviations

AAS	—	Acta Apostolicae Sedis
ADSC	—	Acta et decreta sacrorum Conciliorum recentiorum. Collectio Lacensis
AER	—	The American Ecclesiastical Review
Ang	—	Angelicum
Ant	—	Antonianum
ASC	—	Alma Socia Christi
ASS	—	Acta Sanctae Sedis
ATG	—	Archivo Teológico Granadino
ATh	—	L'Année Théologique
Bibl	—	Biblica
BSFEM	—	Bulletin de la Société Française d'Etudes Mariales
CB	—	Cultura Bíblica
CBQ	—	The Catholic Biblical Quarterly
CBrg	—	Collationes Brugenses
CC	—	Civiltà Cattolica
CFS	—	Collectanea Franciscana Slavica
CM	—	Collectanea Mechliniensia
CSCO	—	Corpus Scriptorum Christianorum Orientalium
CSEL	—	Corpus Scriptorum Ecclesiasticorum Latinorum
CTh	—	Collectanea Theologica
DAFC	—	Dictionnaire Apologétique de la Foi Catholique
DB	—	Enchiridion Symbolorum (Denzinger-Bannwart-Umberg)
DTC	—	Dictionnaire de Théologie Catholique (Vacant-Mangenot)
DTFr	—	Divus Thomas (Freiburg)

DTPl	—	Divus Thomas (Placentia)
EB	—	Enchiridion Biblicum
EE	—	Estudios Eclesiásticos
EF	—	Etudes Franciscaines
EL	—	Ephemerides Liturgicae
EM	—	Estudios Marianos
Eml	—	Emmanuel
EphM	—	Ephemerides Mariologicae
Est	—	Estudios (Mercedarios)
EstF	—	Estudios Franciscanos
ETL	—	Ephemerides Theologicae Lovanienses
FS	—	Franciscan Studies
GCS	—	Die griechischen christlichen Schriftsteller der ersten drei Jahrhunderte
Gr	—	Gregorianum
HPR	—	The Homiletic and Pastoral Review
Mansi	—	Sacrorum Conciliorum nova et amplissima collectio (J. D. Mansi)
Maria (du Manoir)	—	Maria; études sur la Sainte Vierge (H. du Manoir) Vol. 1 (Paris, 1949)
Mariology (Carol)	—	Mariology (ed. J. B. Carol), Vol. 1 (Milwaukee, Wis., 1954), Vol. 2 (1956)
MC	—	Miscellanea Comillas
MF	—	Miscellanea Francescana
Mm	—	Marianum
Mre	—	Marie (Nicolet, Canada)
MS	—	Marian Studies
Mth	—	The Month
NRT	—	Nouvelle Revue Théologique
OC	—	Oriens Christianus
OLD	—	Our Lady's Digest
OssR	—	L'Osservatore Romano
PCTSA	—	Proceedings of the Catholic Theological Society of America
PG	—	Patrologia Graeca (Migne)

PL	—	Patrologia Latina (Migne)
PO	—	Patrologia Orientalis (Graffin-Nau)
RdJ	—	Enchiridion Patristicum (Rouët de Journel)
REB	—	Revista Eclesiástica Brasileira
RHE	—	Revue d'Histoire Ecclésiastique
RSR	—	Recherches de Science Religieuse
RUO	—	Revue de l'Université d'Ottawa
SF	—	Studi Francescani
SM	—	Studia Mariana (Academia Mariana Internationalis, Rome)
Thom	—	The Thomist
ThR	—	Theologische Revue
ThS	—	Theological Studies
TuU	—	Texte und Untersuchungen
VD	—	Verbum Domini
VgI	—	Virgo Immaculata. Acta Congressus Mariologici Mariani Romae anno 1954 celebrati.
VyV	—	Verdad y Vida
ZfkT	—	Zeitschrift für katholische Theologie

Introductory Chapter

FOR pedagogic reasons, the scientific and systematic treatment of any branch of knowledge as such (and hence of Mariology) is generally preceded by a few preliminary notions concerning its adequate object, its nature and importance, its sources, methods and principles. Hence this introductory chapter which will set forth the entire course in its proper perspective. These elementary notions will be followed by a few general observations relative to the contemporary Marian movement which will serve to emphasize the importance and timeliness of this study.

I. *Definition.* By its very definition, Mariology is the study of Mary. More precisely, it is that part of the science of theology which treats of the Mother of God in her singular mission, prerogatives and cult. Its material object, then, is Mary in her relation to the Creator and to His creatures. Its formal object: the light of divine revelation supplying the various truths concerning her, and aiding the human intellect in its attempt to fathom them.

II. *Division.* Here is the general outline of the course we propose to follow:

1

PART I
Mary's Mission

A. Preparation
- (1) Predestination
- (2) Prophecies

B. Fulfillment: The Divine Maternity

C. Corollaries
- (1) Spiritual Maternity
- (2) Universal Mediation
- (3) Universal Queenship

PART II
Mary's Prerogatives

A. Beginning of her life
- (1) Immaculate Conception
- (2) Fullness of grace

B. During her life
- (1) Freedom from Actual Sin
- (2) Perpetual Virginity
- (3) Mary's Knowledge

C. End of her life
- (1) Immunity from Corruption
- (2) Anticipated Resurrection
- (3) Bodily Assumption

D. Corollary: The Cult of Mary.

The division of Mariology varies considerably according to authors. In our treatment of this subject we have adopted what seems to be a scientific and logical division, namely: A) The singular mission to which Mary was divinely chosen, that is, to be the Mother of Christ, the Son of God and our Redeemer. B) The singular prerogatives of soul and body which she received in order to fulfill that mission in a fitting manner. C) The singular cult due to her because of her unique mission and prerogatives. Since this division is not an integral part of the purely dogmatic aspect of Mariology, it is treated in this book as a corollary.

III. *Excellence.* The excellence and importance of Mariology flow logically from its object. Next to God and the sacred Humanity of Christ, Mary is the most noble and perfect of all existing beings, human or angelic. She holds the highest place among creatures in the order of grace and glory. She constitutes a hierarchy of her own between God and man. Because of her central position in the plan of God, the study of her mission and privileges will necessarily widen and deepen our understanding and appreciation of the various other phases of Catholic theology. In a very true sense, Mariology is like a compendium of all other Christian dogmas. Hence, after the study of God Himself, no other study is nobler and more excellent than that of His worthy Mother.

IV. *Sources.* The sources of Mariology, like those of theology in general, are Sacred Scripture and Sacred Tradition. It is in these sources that the scholar endeavors to find the various truths concerning the Mother of God in order to explain them, arrange them into an organic and systematic whole, and draw new conclusions from them through a legitimate process of reasoning.[1]

Marian truths may be found in these sources of revelation either formally (explicitly or implicitly) or virtually. A truth is contained in the sources formally-explicitly if it is stated therein clearly, in express or equivalent terms; formally-implicitly, if our intellect discovers it by analysing the fuller concept of some other truth clearly revealed; virtually, if our intellect arrives at its knowledge by way of a deduction from two other truths, one of which is formally revealed and the other known through natural reason.

While references to Our Blessed Lady in Sacred Scripture are relatively few, they are, nevertheless, very precious and pregnant with meaning. These references are found in some of the Old Testament prophecies (for example: Genesis 3:15; Isaias 7:14; Jeremiah 31:22; Micheas 5:2–3), and particularly in the New Testament account of the Annunciation (Luke 1:26–38), the Visitation (Luke 1:39–56), the angel's apparition to Joseph assuring him of Mary's virginity (Matthew 1:18–25), the birth of Our Lord (Luke 2:1–7), the purification of Mary and the Child's presentation in the temple (Luke 2:22–38), the wedding feast at Cana (John 2:1–11),

[1] Cf. S. Alameda, O.S.B., *La Mariología y las fuentes de la revelación,* in *EM,* 1 (1942), 41–100.

Mary's presence beneath the cross (John 19:25–27), St. Paul's references to the divine Maternity (Galatians 4:4), and St. John's vision of the Woman clothed with the sun (Apocalypse 12:1–18). The systematic study of these and various other biblical passages bearing on Our Lady is called Biblical Mariology, and is receiving more and more attention at the present time.[2]

By Sacred Tradition we mean here the body of revealed truths not contained in the Bible, but transmitted from generation to generation under the guidance of the magisterium or teaching authority of the Church. For the most part, the teaching of Tradition regarding Our Blessed Lady is made known to us, not only through the works of the early Fathers and Doctors of the Church, but likewise through the beliefs of the theologians and the faithful of subsequent centuries, including our own times. It is well known that the teaching of Tradition has played a major role in the progressive development of Mariology; hence its importance cannot be overestimated.[3]

---

[2] Cf. F. Ceuppens, O.P., *De Mariologia biblica*, 2nd ed. (Rome, 1951); E. May, O.F.M.Cap., *Mary in the Old Testament*, in *Mariology* (Carol), 1, 51–79; M. J. Gruenthaner, S.J., *Mary in the New Testament*, ibid., 80–108; D. J. Unger, O.F.M.Cap., *The Use of Sacred Scripture in Mariology*, in *MS*, 1 (1950), 67–116.

[3] Cf. W. J. Burghardt, S.J., *Mary in Western Patristic Thought*, in *Mariology* (Carol), 1, 109–155; Id., *Mary in Eastern Patristic Thought*, ibid., 2, Ch. 3; G. W. Shea, *Outline History of Mariology in the Middle Ages and Modern Times*, ibid., 1, 281–327. A handy collection of Marian texts from the Fathers and some medieval writers may be found in J. Keuppens, M.A., *Mariologiae compendium* (Antwerp, 1938), 182–237.

In order to be valid in theology (and, therefore, in
Mariology) the positive data furnished by both Sacred
Scripture and Tradition must be interpreted in complete
accordance with the directives issued by the magisterium
through its various organs or branches. It is the living and
infallible magisterium of the Church which preserves the
deposit of God's revelation in its original purity, and
authoritatively explains its genuine meaning to us. Consequently, in treating the various mariological theses the
first and last word must always be left to the magisterium,
which is the proximate norm or rule of faith.[4]

The abundant material supplied by the magisterium
concerning Our Blessed Lady is to be found in the
numerous encyclicals and other documents of the Supreme Pontiffs, in the declarations of Ecumenical Councils, in the concordant and universal preaching of the
bishops throughout the world, and in the liturgical books
approved by the Church.[5] Obviously, not all these documents will be equally weighty and decisive. They must
be utilized in specific cases according to the norms
generally accepted in Catholic theology. But as regards
papal pronouncements, whether they contain infallible

[4] Cf. Pius XII's allocution to the International Mariological Congress held in Rome, October 24, 1954, in AAS, 46 (1954), 677–680,
esp. p. 678.

[5] The more important papal and conciliar declarations on Our Lady
may be found in P. Palmer, S.J., *Mary in the Documents of the
Church* (Westminster, Md., 1952), and in Doheny-Kelly, *Papal Docu-
ments on Mary* (Milwaukee, Wis., 1954). Cf. likewise E. Carroll,
O.Carm., *Mary in the Documents of the Magisterium*, in *Mariology*
(Carol), 1, 1–50. For the Liturgy, cf. C. Gumbinger, O.F.M.Cap.,
Mary in the Eastern Liturgies, ibid., 185–244; and S. Daly, O.S.B.,
Mary in the Western Liturgy, ibid., 245–280.

declarations or not, they deserve the theologians' humble respect and acceptance.[6]

V. *Primary Principle.* By "primary principle" we mean a fundamental truth which furnishes the ultimate reason for the various theses of a given science. In other words, it is a basic proposition, accepted by all, which alone gives organic coherence and logical nexus to the whole treatise. Since Mariology is a true science (although subordinate to the general science of theology), it follows that it should have such a fundamental principle.[7] However, theologians disagree widely as to what exactly constitutes this primary or basic proposition. Their opinions may be summarized as follows:

A. According to a large number of authors, the fundamental principle of Mariology is the divine Maternity. In their opinion, this truth: "Mary is the Mother of God," contains in germ all the other prerogatives which we predicate of her; it is the truth that gives stability and coherence to the whole edifice of Mariology.[8]

B. According to a small group of authors, the basic truth of all Mariology is the doctrine of Our Lady's role as Second Eve or Coredemptrix. Everything else in Mari-

---

[6] Cf. J. C. Fenton, *The Lesson of "Humani generis,"* in AER, 123 (1950), 359–378; E. D. Benard, *The Doctrinal Value of the Ordinary Teaching of the Holy Father in View of "Humani generis,"* in PCTSA, 6 (1951), 78–107.

[7] Cf. C. Vollert, S.J., *The Scientific Structure of Mariology,* in Mariology (Carol), 2, Ch. 1.

[8] Cf. C. Vollert, S.J., *The Fundamental Principle of Mariology,* ibid. Ch. 2; M. Llamera, O.P., *La Maternidad espiritual de María,* in EM, 3 (1944), 162; M. R. Gagnebet, O.P., *Questions mariales,* in Ang, 22 (1945), 165 f.

ology, they claim, may be logically deduced from that role. Even the divine Maternity was conferred on Mary as a means to the proper fulfillment of that mission.[9]

C. Others, believing that neither of the above truths alone can account for every other Marian prerogative, postulate *two* fundamental principles, namely: "Mary is the Mother of God" and "Mary is the Second Eve or Coredemptrix."[10]

D. A fourth group of theologians contends that the fundamental principle is formally one, but virtually complex. It consists, according to the various authors of this group, in:

(1) "The Bridal Maternity of Mary."[11] By this they mean that, in the present economy, Our Lady is not only the Mother of Christ, but at the same time and by that very fact, His mystical bride in the spiritual regeneration of mankind.

(2) "The divine Maternity taken concretely."[12] That is to say, the divine Maternity, not in its purely abstract concept, but as it actually took place in the present

[9] S. Alameda, *El primer principio mariológico según los Padres*, in EM, 3 (1944), 163–186; L. P. Everett, C.SS.R., *The Nexus between Mary's Coredemptive Role and Her Other Prerogatives*, in MS, 2 (1951), 140–142.

[10] J. Bittremieux, *De principio supremo Mariologiae*, in ETL, 8 (1931), 250 f; J. Keuppens, *Mariologiae compendium* (Antwerp, 1938), 12.

[11] M. J. Scheeben, *Handbuch der katholischen Dogmatik*, 3 (Freiburg i. Br., 1882), 489; E. Druwé, S.J., *Position et structure du traité marial*, in BSFEM, 2 (1936), 23; C. Feckes, *Das Fundamentalprinzip der Mariologie*, in Scientia Sacra (Köln-Düsseldorf, 1935), 252–276.

[12] J. M. Bover, S.J., *Síntesis orgánica de la Mariología en función de la asociación de María a la obra redentora de Jesucristo* (Madrid, 1929), esp. 10–12.

historical order, namely, as necessarily implying Our Lady's cooperation with Christ in the Redemption and spiritual regeneration of mankind. This opinion substantially coincides with that of the first group mentioned above.

(3) "The Universal Motherhood of Mary," namely, Mary simultaneously the Mother of God, of angels and of men (according to Roschini); or again "Mary is the Mother of the Whole Christ" (according to García Garcés). In other words, Mary is the physical Mother of the Head (Christ) and simultaneously the spiritual Mother of the members.[13]

A few other views have been recently expressed in this connection, such as that of Father Semmelroth, according to whom the primary principle of Mariology would be: "Mary is the type and personification of the Church," and that of A. Müller who claims that the basis of all Mariology is Our Lady's plenitude of grace.[14] The future will tell whether these views are such that they can win a fair number of adherents. As to our personal preference, we endorse the first opinion mentioned above (i.e., in favor of the divine Maternity) as being more in accordance with the mind of the Church.[15]

VI. *Contemporary Mariological Movement.* By mari-

[13] G. M. Roschini, O.S.M., *La Madonna secondo la fede e la teologia,* 1 (Rome, 1953), 112–116; N. García Garcés, C.M.F., *Mater Coredemptrix* (Turin, 1940), 121–123.

[14] O. Semmelroth, S. J., *Urbild der Kirche* (Würzburg, 1950), 37–39; A. Müller, *Um die Grundlagen der Mariologie,* in *DTFr,* 29 (1951), 389. For further references on this entire question cf. Vollert, *art. cit.*

[15] Pius XII, *Fulgens corona,* in *AAS,* 45 (1953), 580.

ological movement we mean, in general, the more or less
concerted endeavor of the Catholic clergy and laity to
promote a deeper appreciation of Our Lady's prerogatives
and thereby increase our devotion to her.[16] By their very
nature, the various manifestations of this organized effort
may be said to fall under two different headings: one
speculative or theological, the other practical or devotional. The latter, which would include such items as
pilgrimages, activities of Marian Sodalities, Legion of
Mary, books, pamphlets and meetings calculated to foster
Marian piety, is not of direct concern to us here. The
former (i.e., the theological aspect) deserves our special
attention inasmuch as it reveals to us in a tangible
manner the tremendous progress made by the science of
Mariology in recent years, and the immediate causes of
that progress.

It may be safely stated that the contemporary mariological movement now under consideration owes its
origin and inspiration to the dogmatic definition of the
Immaculate Conception in the year 1854. It is now
generally conceded that the scientific treatment of
Mariology, as we know it today, is the logical outgrowth
of that epoch-making papal pronouncement. It was the
impetus given in this direction first by Pius IX, and later
on by Leo XIII through his immortal Marian encyclicals,
that stimulated Catholic theologians to devote greater

[16] Cf. J. B. Carol, O.F.M., *The Mariological Movement in the World Today*, in MS, 1 (1950), 25–45.

attention to this noble branch of the sacred sciences. Nor did the encouragement of the Holy See in any way diminish after Leo XIII. The numerous encyclicals and other documents issued by St. Pius X, Benedict XV, Pius XI and Pius XII have continued to prove a source of inspiration to the Catholic student in his eagerness to broaden his knowledge of the Marian prerogatives and to correlate them in an organic synthesis.[17]

Besides the magisterium, another factor which has contributed considerably to the progress of Mariology has been the critical edition of innumerable patristic writings and liturgical texts, particularly the Oriental Patrology prepared by Graffin-Nau, the Berlin edition of the Greek Fathers, the Vienna edition of the Latin Fathers, the Greek and Latin Patrology edited by Migne, and the Blume-Dreves collection of medieval liturgical and quasi-liturgical hymns.[18] These and various other publications of a similar nature constitute an inexhaustible fund of material which has made it possible for contemporary scholars to reconstruct a positive Mariology on a scientific basis, and to eliminate a good

[17] Cf. E. Carroll, *art. cit.*
[18] *Patrologia Orientalis*, ed. Graffin-Nau (Paris, 1903 ff), 26 vols. so far; *Die griechischen christlichen Schriftsteller der ersten drei Jahrhunderte* (Leipzig, 1897 ff), 41 vols.; *Corpus scriptorum ecclesiasticorum latinorum* (Vienna, 1866 ff), 74 vols.; *Patrologiae cursus completus; series latina*, ed. Migne (Paris, 1844–1855), 217 vols.; id., *series graeca* (Paris, 1857–1866), 162 vols.; *Texte und Untersuchungen zur Geschichte der altchristlichen Literatur* (Leipzig, 1882 ff), 41 vols.; *Analecta hymnica medii aevi*, ed. Blume-Dreves (Leipzig, 1886–1922), 55 vols.

deal of spurious documentation much exploited in the past.[19]

Among the multiple evidences of the vigorous renaissance and vitality of Marian studies in this period, we may single out the following:

A. The impressive series of *Marian Congresses*, both national and international, beginning in the city of Livorno (Italy) in 1895, and continuing down to the present day with ever-increasing frequency.[20] The most important of these, from a theological point of view, are undoubtedly the ones organized by the International Marian Academy, headed by Father C. Balić, O.F.M., in Rome, and published under the titles *Studia Mariana* and *Alma Socia Christi*. The former set, in eight volumes and mostly on the Assumption, contains the dissertations read at the Congresses held in Rome (1947), Lisbon (1947), Madrid (1947), Montreal (1948), Buenos Aires (1948), Le Puy (1949), and Washington, D.C. (1950).[21] The latter set, in 12 volumes, gathers the papers and discussions of the International Marian Congress held in Rome in 1950.[22]

B. The founding of *Mariological Academies* such as

[19] A very valuable list of non-authentic patristic and medieval works dealing with Our Lady has been recently published by R. Laurentin as an appendix to his *Court traité de théologie mariale* (Paris, 1953), 119–173.

[20] Cf. E. Campana, *Maria nel culto cattolico*, 2nd ed., 2 (Turin, 1943), 487–652; Roschini, *Mariologia*, 2nd ed., 2, part 3 (Rome, 1948), 185–189.

[21] Cf. Carol, *Recent Literature on Mary's Assumption*, in AER, 120 (1949), 376–387.

[22] The two sets may be procured through the *Academia Internazionale Mariana*, Via Merulana, 124, Rome, Italy.

the Pontifical Roman Academy of the Immaculate Conception in 1835, and the International Marian Academy organized by Father Balić in Rome in 1946;[23] the establishment of national *Mariological Societies*[24] in Belgium (1931), in France (1934), in Spain (1940), in Canada (1948), in the United States of America (1950), in Belgium for the French-speaking public (1951), and finally in Germany (1952); the founding of *Marian Centers,* such as the International Marian Center of the Servite Fathers in Rome (1938), the Marian Franciscan Commission in Rome, headed by Father Balić (1946), and the Canadian Marian Center in Nicolet, organized by M. Roger Brien (1948); the establishment of chairs for special courses in Mariology in Washington, D.C. (1918), and in various universities and houses of theology in Rome and elsewhere.[25]

C. The gathering together of Marian sources and other literature in *Marian Libraries* to facilitate and stimulate research among students of Mariology. The more important of these libraries are: the one in the International College of the Servites in Rome, reorganized in 1943 by Fathers G. M. Roschini and G. M. Besutti, O.S.M.; the one in Banneux, Belgium (1942) under the direction of Abbé L. Arendt; in the University of Dayton, Ohio,

---

[23] Cf. C. Balić, O.F.M., *Il contributo dei Frati Minori al movimento mariologico moderno,* in Mm, 11 (1949), 441–460; L. Di Fonzo, O.F.M.Conv., *L'Academie Pontificale de l'Immaculée à Rome,* in Mre, 7, n. 4 (1953), 73–75.

[24] Cf. Carol, *art. cit.,* in MS, 1 (1950), 27–28.

[25] Cf. W. P. Kennedy, *National Shrine of the Immaculate Conception,* 1 (Washington, D.C., 1927), 263–264.

organized in 1943 by Father L. W. Monheim, S.M.; in the National Shrine of the Immaculate Conception, Washington, D.C., originally started by Msgr. B. Mc-Kenna; in the Marist Brothers' Scholasticate, Poughkeepsie, New York, under the direction of Brother Cyril Robert, F.M.S. To these may be added the author's private collection (now kept in New York City), which is particularly rich from a theological point of view.[26]

D. Finally, the publication of scientific magazines exclusively devoted to Mariology. The first to appear was *Marianum*, a quarterly edited by the Servite Fathers in Rome since 1939. It has been followed, since 1951, by *Ephemerides Mariologicae*, published by the Claretian Fathers in Madrid. Under this heading we may recall also, as deserving of special mention, the proceedings of the annual conventions of the various Mariological Societies mentioned above, namely: *Mariale Dagen*, of the Flemish Mariological Society, since 1933; *Bulletin de la Société Française d'Etudes Mariales*, of the French Mariology Society, since 1935 (except 1939–1947); *Estudios Marianos*, of the Spanish Mariological Society, since 1942; *Marian Studies*, of the Mariological Society of America, since 1950; and the *Journées sacerdotales mariales*, of the French-speaking Mariological Society of Belgium, since 1952.[27]

From the preceding survey, although sketchy and superficial, it is sufficiently clear that Mariology has

---

[26] Cf. L. W. Monheim, S.M., *Some Marian Collections in the World*, in MS, 1 (1950), 46–55.

[27] Cf. Carol, *art. cit.*, 27–28.

ceased to be a mere "appendix" to the tract on the Incarnation, and has become a highly important theological treatise in itself. The impressive development it has undergone in recent decades, and the ever-increasing attention it is receiving from contemporary scholars constitute a consoling presage of even further progress and achievements in the future.[28]

Select Bibliography

For the benefit of those wishing to make a further and more detailed study of the various theological questions concerning Our Blessed Lady, we list here a few of the standard general works on the subject. Publications dealing with specific problems will be indicated at the opportune time in the course of this book.

In English:

Canice, Fr., O.F.M. Cap., *Mary: A Study of the Mother of God* (Dublin, M. H. Gill & Son, 1937).

Carol, J. B., O.F.M. (ed.), *Mariology*, Vol. 1 (Milwaukee, Wis., Bruce, 1954).

Garrigou-Lagrange, R., O.P., *The Mother of the Saviour and Our Interior Life* (St. Louis, Mo., Herder, 1949).

James, Fr., O.F.M. Cap., *The Mother of Jesus* (Westminster, Md., The Newman Bookshop, 1946).

Marian Studies, published annually (since 1950) by The Mariological Society of America, Washington, D.C.

[28] Cf Shea, *art. cit.*, esp. 315–327, and the excellent survey—of particular interest for Americans—by C. Vollert, S.J., *Le mouvement mariologique aux Etats-Unis*, in *Maria* (du Manoir), 3, 593–614.

Most, W. G., *Mary in Our Life* (New York, P. J. Kenedy & Sons, 1954).

Neubert, E., S.M., *Mary in Doctrine* (Milwaukee, Wis., Bruce, 1954).

Philipon, M. M., O.P., *The Mother of God* (Westminster, Md., The Newman Bookshop, 1953).

Pohle-Preuss, *Mariology* (St. Louis, Mo., Herder, 1926).

Resch, P., S.M., *Our Blessed Mother. Outlines of Mariology* (Milwaukee, Wis., Bruce, 1939).

Scheeben-Geukers, *Mariology*, 2 vols. (St. Louis, Mo., Herder, 1946–1947).

In French:

D'Alès, A., S.J., art. *Marie*, in *DAFC*, 3, 115–209.

Dublanchy, E., S.M., art. *Marie*, in *DTC*, 9, 2339–2474.

Du Manoir, H., S.J., (ed.), *Maria: Etudes sur la Sainte Vierge*, 3 vols. (Paris, Beauchesne, 1949–1954).

Neubert, E., S.M., *Marie dans le dogme*, 2nd ed. (Paris, 1946).

Terrien, J. B., S. J., *La Mère de Dieu et la Mère des hommes*, 4 vols. (Paris, Lethielleux, 1950).

In Italian:

Bertetto, D., S.D.B., *Maria nel dogma cattolico* (Turin, 1950).

Campana, E., *Maria nel dogma*, 4th ed. (Turin, 1936).

Roschini, G. M., O.S.M., *La Madonna nella fede e la teologia*, 4 vols. (Rome, F. Ferrari, 1953–1954).

Spiazzi, R., O.P. (ed.), *Theotokos. Enciclopedia Mariana* (Milan, 1954).

In Latin:

Aldama, J. de, S.J., *Mariologia*, in the third volume of the
     Sacrae Theologiae Summa, edited by the Spanish Jesuits
     (Madrid, B.A.C., 1950).

Boyer, C., S.J., *Synopsis praelectionum de B. Maria Virgine*
     (Rome, Gregorian University, 1952).

Keuppens, J., W.F., *Mariologiae compendium* (Antwerp,
     1938).

Lépicier, A.H.M., O.S.M., *Tractatus de Beatissima Virgine
     Maria Matre Dei*, 5th. ed. (Rome, 1926).

Merkelbach, H. B., O.P., *Mariologia* (Paris, Desclée, 1939).

Roschini, G. M., O.S.M., *Mariologia*, 4 vols., 2nd ed. (Rome,
     F. Ferrari, 1947–1948).

THE SINGULAR MISSION OF MARY

As indicated in the introductory chapter, the singular mission which God entrusted to Mary was to be the worthy Mother of His Son, the Redeemer of the world. This is the end which God had in view when decreeing the existence of Our Blessed Lady. It constitutes her greatest prerogative, and indeed the basis of all the wonderful privileges which God bestowed upon her. This unique mission of Mary may be considered: (a) in the eternal decree of predestination; (b) in the manifestation of this decree through the prophecies; (c) in its actual fulfillment; and (d) in its immediate consequences. Hence this first part of Mariology may be conveniently divided into the following chapters:

19

CHAPTER ONE

The Predestination of Mary

IN GOD there is neither past nor future, nor succession of time. Everything is eternally present to Him. The complete chain of events taking place in time was foreseen by Him, and willed (or permitted) by Him from all eternity. If, in point of time, we find Our Blessed Lady fulfilling a specific mission entrusted to her by the Almighty, it is obvious that this mission is the result of a positive act on the part of God's will from all eternity. This divine will determining the existence of Our Lady, ordaining her to the beatific vision and (as a means to the end) charging her with a specific function in the divine economy is what we mean here by her predestination.

The teaching of Mariologists concerning the various phases of Mary's predestination may be summarized in the following four propositions. The first two are accepted by all; the third and fourth are peculiar to the followers of the Franciscan School.

First Proposition: The Blessed Virgin was predestined to be the Mother of God by an absolutely gratuitous act on the part of God. That means that Our Lady did not merit this Maternity *in the order of intention,* as the Schoolmen say. The reason is that the divine Maternity was the very source of all her merit, and hence could not

21

be the object of any merit on her part. However, theologians generally admit that Mary merited the divine Maternity in the order of execution; not in strict justice, but only out of fittingness. In other words, once God had decreed to make Mary the Mother of His Son, He gave her the grace to merit that high degree of sanctity and purity which would render her worthy to be the Mother of God.[29]

Second Proposition: The Blessed Virgin was predestined to the divine Maternity in one and the same decree with Christ. This is the teaching of Pius IX in the bull *Ineffabilis Deus* (December 8, 1854), and of Pius XII in the bull *Munificentissimus Deus* (November 1, 1950). Both state unequivocally that Jesus and Mary were predestined "uno eodemque decreto."[30] This may be gathered also from Sacred Scripture. If the Bible, from Genesis to Apocalypse, shows Christ and Mary always indissolubly united in the fulfillment of one and the same mission, we may rightly presume that they were predestined together. Reason confirms this, for the terms "mother" and "son" are so correlative that one necessarily calls for the other.

Third Proposition: With and under Christ, the Blessed Virgin was predestined with a logical priority to all others. It is true that God predestined all rational crea-

[29] *Summa Theologica*, III, 2, 11, ad 3.
[30] Pius IX, in ADSC, 6 (Friburgi Brisgoviae, 1882), 836; Pius XII, in AAS, 42 (1950), 768. Cf. Th. Plassmann, O.F.M., *Uno eodemque decreto. Maria Immaculata praedestinata in Sacra Pagina*, in Vgl 3 (Rome, 1955) 174–197.

tures from all eternity in one single decree. Nevertheless, in this one single decree the human mind ought to distinguish several virtual decrees (or logical stages of the one decree) affecting various persons according to the laws of reasonable order and hierarchy. "That which is better in the effects, is prior in the intention of the agent."[31] Sacred Scriptures speak of Wisdom as being "the firstborn before all creatures," created from the beginning and before the centuries (Ecclesiasticus 24:1–15). The "Wisdom" spoken of here is the Incarnate Wisdom (i.e., Christ), as we learn from the Epistles of St. Paul (I Corinthians 24:30; Colossians 1:15ff; 2:3; Hebrews 1:2). It is only in the light of this that we may truthfully speak of Christ as holding an absolute and universal primacy over all creatures. Since Mother and Son were predestined in one and the same decree, it follows that the above reasoning applies also—with proper subordination—to Our Blessed Lady. Consequently, her predestination (the same as Christ's) could not have been conditioned upon that of Adam and Eve or any other creature. It was rather the other way around.[32]

[31] St. Thomas, *Contra Gentiles*, 2, 44, 1; cf. Scotus, *Op. oxon.*, lib. 3, d. 7, q. 3; in *J. D. Scoti Theologiae Marianae elementa*, ed. C. Balić, O.F.M. (Sibenici, 1933), 5.

[32] For the opposite view, held by the Thomistic School, cf. W. Allen, *The Predestination of Mary in the Light of Modern Controversy*, in MS, 2 (1951), 178–192.

According to the theory elaborated in recent years by the eminent French theologian, Fr. J.-F. Bonnefoy, O.F.M., the various logical stages which make up the one single decree of predestination bearing on the Incarnation and Redemption ought to be arranged in the following manner: *First*, God decrees the Incarnation of His only begotten Son for its intrinsic perfection, and as the highest possible communication of His own goodness and happiness (cf. *Summa theologica*, III, 1, 1).

Fourth Proposition: The predestination of the Blessed Virgin was the secondary cause of the predestination of all others. This thesis is a necessary corollary of the above. Christ is the primary exemplary cause of our predestination, as we gather from St. Paul: "For those whom he has foreknown, he has also predestined to become conformed to the image of his Son" (Romans 8:29). Christ is likewise the efficient cause of our predestination because He merited it for us. Lastly, He is the final cause

---

Second, God decrees Mary, Christ's Associate, so that Christ may have a most perfect beneficiary with whom He may share His own goodness and happiness. *Third,* God decrees the angels and men, so that Christ and Mary may have beneficiaries on whom they may bestow their gifts. *Fourth,* since it is more noble to dispense one's own gifts than those of others, God decrees that Christ and Mary will *merit* such gifts for their beneficaries. *Fifth,* since the most excellent way to show one's love is to lay down one's life for the loved ones, God decrees Christ's redemptive passion and death, with Mary's intimate share therein. *Sixth,* since it is more noble and perfect to forgive than to give, God decrees (with a permissive will) the fall of our first parents, so as to make possible the Redemption (and Coredemption) from sin. — In order to appraise the above perspective, it is necessary to bear in mind the principles and reasoning process utilized by the author in his extensive article *La primauté absolue et universelle de N. S. Jésu-Christ et de la Très-Sainte Vierge,* in FSFEM, 4 (1939), 43–98. Cf. also his article *The Predestination of Our Blessed Lady,* in Mariology (Carol), 2, Ch. 4; and *Sa Sainteté Pie XII et la primauté du Christ et de la T.S. Vierge,* in SF, 12 (1940), 2–6. Bonnefoy's theory has been partially endorsed by Roschini. Nevertheless, the latter still insists that the primary reason of the Incarnation is God's free election of the present order in which the Incarnation is connected with (not dependent on) the sin of Adam. Cf. Rocca-Roschini, *De ratione primaria existentiae Christi et Deiparae* (Rome, 1944); Roschini, *Intorno alla questione sul cosidetto motivo dell'Incarnazione,* in MF, 48 (1948), 296–305. Obviously, Roschini fails to see that he has left the fundamental question unanswered, namely: *why* did God freely choose the present order from among other possible orders? He could have found an excellent starting point in the declaration of the Vatican Council to the effect that God created everything in order to manifest and share His infinite goodness and happiness. Cf. Conc. Vat., sessio 3, de fide, c. 1; ADSC, 7 (Friburgi-Brisgoviae, 1892), 250.

of our predestination inasmuch as we are all predestined for His honor and glory.[33] Now, since the Blessed Virgin shares the primacy of Christ in the eternal decrees of God, she must share also the causality of her Son with regard to all others. In other words, we are all indebted to her, after Christ, for our own predestination.[34]

[33] *Summa theologica,* I, 105, 5: "That which is imperfect is ordained to that which is more perfect."

[34] Cf. Bonnefoy, *Le mérite social de Marie et sa prédestination,* in *ASC,* 2, 21–48, esp. 32 ff.

CHAPTER TWO

Mary in the Prophecies

FOR centuries before Our Blessed Lord was actually born, Almighty God had sought to prepare the Chosen People for that extraordinary event by raising up holy men who, at various times and in His name, would foretell certain important facts concerning the future Messias, and would thus keep alive the hope of fallen mankind in their future Redeemer. In some of these Old Testament prophecies reference is made not only to the person of the Redeemer Himself, but also—quite understandably—to His Blessed Mother. From the Mariologist's point of view, the most important of these prophetic passages are the Protoevangelium (Genesis 3:15) and the oracle concerning the Virgin-Mother of the Savior (Isaias 7:14).[35]

Article 1

THE PROTOEVANGELIUM

The word "Protoevangelium" (or First Gospel) means literally "the first good news" and is used to designate the oldest biblical prophecy foreshadowing the future Redeemer. Its text and context may be briefly sum-

[35] For other Old Testament passages with reference to Our Lady, cf. E. May, *art. cit.*, 65–79.

marized as follows. Immediately after the fall of our first parents, through whom the serpent had won a victory over the human race using Eve as an instrument of his evil designs, God Himself addresses the serpent and foretells his punishment and utter defeat through the instrumentality of a "woman" and "her seed." God's words to the tempter were: "I will put enmities between thee and the woman, between thy seed and her seed; he (the woman's seed) shall crush thy head, and thou shalt lie in wait for his heel."[36] In order to understand the full implications of this prophecy we must try to identify the principals in the struggle and victory predicted by God, namely, the serpent, the seed of the serpent, the seed of the woman, and the woman herself.

I. *The Serpent*. According to the Rationalists, the serpent addressed by God in the garden of Eden was the physical animal of that name. Hence the enmities predicted in the text refer only to the instinctive repugnance which men feel toward all reptiles. However, according to all Catholic commentators, the serpent was actually Satan himself who had taken on the appearance of a reptile. The Catholic interpretation is confirmed by other passages in the Bible, for example, the Book of Wisdom 2:24: "By the envy of the devil, death came into the world."

II. *The Seed of the Serpent*. According to non-Catholics, the seed of the serpent represents all other physical

[36] The Vulgate differs from the original Hebrew text, among other things, in that it attributes the crushing of the serpent's head directly to the woman.

reptiles. According to Catholics, it stands for sin itself,[37] or for all the devils, or again for all evil men.[38]

III. *The Seed of the Woman.* According to Catholic commentators, the word "seed" here should be understood either in an individual sense, referring to Christ alone, or in a collective sense, referring to the whole posterity of Eve, but with Christ implied in a special manner.[39] We believe that the first of these opinions should be preferred. The main reason is that, as we know from experience, all men and women are not, and never have been, at enmity with the devil. Furthermore, as we know from subsequent revelation, Christ and Christ *alone* (not the posterity of Eve) utterly crushed the head of the devil by redeeming the human race from the servitude of sin.[40] The posterity of Eve was the beneficiary of that victory, not its agent.

IV. *The Woman.* There are at least five opinions on the matter:[41]

A. The Woman of Genesis 3:15 is Eve and Eve alone. This opinion is held by non-Catholics and also by a few Catholics.

B. The Woman refers to the whole feminine sex, though with special reference to one among them, i.e., Mary. This opinion is held by a few Catholic scholars.

[37] Cf. F. X. Peirce, S.J., *The Protoevangelium,* in CBQ, 13 (1951), 248.
[38] F. Ceuppens, *op. cit.,* 3.
[39] Cf. D. J. Unger, *The First Gospel: Genesis 3:15* (St. Bonaventure, N.Y., 1954), 282–285, where he lists the advocates of both views.
[40] Cf. John 12:31–33; Colossians 2:14–15; Hebrews 2:14–15. Cf. also EB, 334.
[41] For the advocates of each opinion, cf. Unger, *op. cit.,* 285–294.

C. The Woman is Eve in the literal sense, and Mary in the typical sense. This view has quite a few supporters.

D. The Woman stands for both Eve and Mary; for Eve in an imperfect literal sense; for Mary in a perfect or fuller literal sense. This is held by many interpreters.

E. The Woman is Mary alone in an exclusive literal sense. This view has many adherents among Catholic exegetes and theologians. It is also the author's own view, for it seems to be more in accordance with the magisterium of the Church, and also with the text and context of the prophecy itself.

(a) *The Magisterium of the Church.* In the Apostolic Constitution *Ineffabilis Deus* Pope Pius IX uses the Protoevangelium as a biblical argument in favor of Mary's Immaculate Conception.[42] According to a special commission of scholars charged by the Pope to prepare the text of that bull, the Immaculate Conception has a solid basis in the *words* themselves of the Protoevangelium.[43] Hence the document supposes that "the woman" of Genesis 3:15 designates Our Blessed Lady in a *literal* sense. More recently, in the bull *Munificentissimus Deus*,[44] and again in the encyclical *Fulgens Corona*, Pius XII, too, adduces the Protoevangelium as a biblical

---

[42] Cf. *ADSC*, 6, 839. On this point see our extensive commentary in *De Corredemptione B. V. Mariae disquisitio positiva* (Vatican City, 1950), 100–121.

[43] Cf. V. Sardi, *La solenne definizione del dogma dell'Immacolato Concepimento di Maria Santissima. Atti e documenti . . . , 1* (Rome, 1905), 796.

[44] AAS, 42 (1950), 768–769.

argument in favor of the Assumption and the Immaculate Conception, respectively.[45]

(b) *The Text and Context.* The text and context of the Protoevangelium lead us to believe that God is here predicting a future, perpetual and absolute enmity between the woman and the devil, and that this struggle or enmity will eventually culminate in the utter destruction of Satan's empire. Surely, none of this applies to Eve who was a friend of Satan and who, in the subsequent pages of Sacred Scripture (Ecclesiasticus 25:33; II Corinthians 11:3; I Timothy 2:14) is always portrayed as such. Besides, the woman of this prophecy is shown as intimately sharing the victory of her seed over the infernal foe.[46] This victory, as we learn from later revelation, is embodied in the redemptive work wrought by Christ.[47] Since Mary, not Eve, was Christ's co-worker in the process of Redemption, we have a right to conclude that she is "the woman" referred to in Genesis 3:15.

Our view is further confirmed by the following observation. Those who identify "the woman" with Eve give as a reason the fact that God wished to punish Satan by predicting his defeat through the very same person used by him to bring about the original fall, namely Eve. This, they claim, would considerably increase the devil's humiliation, and at the same time strengthen the hope and consolation of Eve's posterity.

To this we answer: If God had wished to follow that

[45] AAS, 45 (1953), 579.
[46] Pius XII, *Munificentissimus Deus*, in AAS, 42 (1950), 769.
[47] See references in footnote 40. Cf. Carol, *op. cit.*, 113–116.

pattern, He should have predicted Satan's defeat, not through Eve, but rather through Adam who was, after all, the chief agent in the perpetration of the first sin, and also the physical head of the human race. And yet, if the above interpretation were correct, we should have to exclude Adam entirely from the subsequent victory, for the simple reason that the victory is predicted of the woman and her seed, and Adam is not included in either.

Hence we conclude: the first messianic prophecy, particularly when understood in the light of later revelation and the teaching of the Church, does foretell the mission of the future Redeemer and also that of His Blessed Mother. Her close association with the Messias is based on the fact that she is to be His Mother.[48] The further and more detailed mariological implications of this important oracle will be pointed out when dealing with each specific thesis.

Article 2

THE VIRGIN-MOTHER OF EMMANUEL
(Isaias 7:14)

In the year 732 B.C. Ahaz, king of Juda, being attacked by the kings of Damascus and Israel, was extremely concerned over the lot of his kingdom and the city of Jerusalem. God sent to him the prophet Isaias

---

[48] Cf. B. J. LeFrois, S.V.D., *The Theme of the Divine Maternity in the Scriptures*, in MS, 6 (1955), esp. 103–105.

with the promise of safety, and the latter invited Ahaz
to ask God for a sign or miracle as a pledge of this
promise. The king, under false pretense of piety, refused
to ask for a sign. Then Isaias said: "Therefore the Lord
himself shall give you a sign. Behold a virgin shall conceive and bear a son, and his name shall be called Emmanuel" (Isaias 7:14). The prophecy, in substance, foretells the preservation of the House of David against the
hostility of the two kings, in view of the fact that from
that house or stock the Messias will come miraculously,
that is, through a virginal conception and birth. The
various interpretations of this prophecy, as proposed by
scholars, may be summarized as follows:

I. According to non-Catholics, the "Emmanuel"
mentioned in the text refers to king Ezechias, son of
Ahaz; or to Jasub, the son of Isaias himself; or again to
some other boy not specified. They also claim that "the
virgin" spoken of in the prophecy is the wife of king
Ahaz; or the wife of Isaias; or again some unmarried
woman not specified.

This interpretation is false because, at the time of the
prophecy, Ezechias was already nine years old; and as to
Jasub, the things that are said about "Emmanuel" a
little further on (9:6–7) simply do not fit him. Besides,
Pope Pius VI condemned the opinion of those who denied the messianic character of the oracle in question.[49]

II. According to a few Catholic commentators (for
example, Lamy, Calmet, etc.) "Emmanuel" is literally

[49] Cf. *EB*, 59.

the son of Isaias, but as a type of the future Messias; "the virgin" is literally the wife of Isaias, but as a type of Our Lady. This interpretation, though never condemned by the Church, is likewise false, for a married woman can hardly be the type of a virgin who conceives miraculously.

III. Most Catholics interpret "Emmanuel" and "the virgin" as designating Christ and Mary, respectively, both in a literal sense. Their interpretation finds abundant support in subsequent revelation. Thus, for example, we learn from the gospel of St. Matthew (1:22–23) that the virginal conception of Christ was a direct fulfillment of the prophecy of Isaias. The unanimous consensus of the Fathers and ecclesiastical writers of the Church likewise endorses this interpretation. Furthermore, it is confirmed by the fact that in Isaias 8:8–9 "Emmanuel" is described as the future Savior of his people. Surely, this applies only to Christ. Hence the prophecy refers to Mary's virginity and to her divine Motherhood.

It may be objected that in the original Hebrew text the word for "virgin" is not *bethula* (i.e., a virgin in the technical sense), but *almah* which means simply a "young maiden." Hence there appears to be no argument here in favor of Mary's virginity. Besides, even if she were a virgin in the strict sense, the very fact that she later conceived and bore a son would automatically destroy her previous virginity.

To this we may answer that, although the term *almah*, taken etymologically, does not necessarily designate a virgin in the technical sense, nevertheless in the other six biblical passages in which that term is used (for example, Genesis 24:43; Exodus 2:8; Canticles 1:2 and 6; Psalm 68:26; and Proverbs 30:18–19) virginity in the strict sense is implied. Furthermore, it must be recalled that the Hebrew text does not say: "Behold a virgin *shall* conceive and bear a son . . . ," but more exactly and literally: "Behold the virgin (is) pregnant and (is) bearing a son . . ." In other words, the young maiden is described by the prophet as retaining her virginity *while* conceiving and bearing her offspring.[50]

[50] Cf. S. Bonano, C.M.F., *Ecce Virgo concipiet et pariet Filium* (*Isaias: 7:14*). *Text and Context*, in *EphM*, 4 (1954); 89–115; May, *art. cit.*, 62–65.

CHAPTER THREE

Mary, the Mother of God

HAVING considered Our Blessed Lady in her predestination and in the prophetic utterances of the Old Testament, let us now turn to the realization, in point of time, of the unique mission assigned to her by the Almighty, namely, to be the worthy Mother of the Son of God.[51] In treating this subject we will discuss briefly:

    I. the errors in this connection;
    II. the official teaching of the Church;
    III. the argument from Sacred Scripture;
    IV. the teaching of Tradition;
    V. the theological explanation of the Catholic dogma;
    VI. the objective dignity resulting from it.

I. *Errors Concerning the Divine Maternity.* The Docetae, Anabaptists, and other heretics held that Christ was true God, but not a true man; hence, in their opinion, Mary could not be said to have begotten Him. On the contrary, the Ebionites, Arians, Rationalists and others hold that Christ was a true man, but not God; hence, Mary may be called the Mother of Christ, but in no

[51] On this chapter cf. Roschini, *op. cit.*, 2, part 1, 141–195; A. d'Alès, S.J., art. *Marie*, in DAFC, 3, 199–206; C. Feckes, *The Mystery of the Divine Motherhood* (London, 1941); Pohle-Preuss, *Mariology*, 5th ed. (St. Louis, Mo., 1926), 4–23; G. Van Ackeren, S.J., *Mary's Divine Motherhood*, in *Mariology* (Carol), 2 Ch. 5.

35

way the Mother of God. The third error is that of the Nestorians, who claim that there were two persons in Christ (one divine and one human), and that Mary gave birth only to the human person; therefore, she cannot be called Mother of God.

II. *The Official Teaching of the Church.* The Third General Council of the Church, which met in Ephesus in the year 431, under the presidency of St. Cyril of Alexandria, unhesitatingly approved the latter's second letter to Nestorius in which the Blessed Virgin is openly proclaimed as *Theotokos* (i.e. Mother of God).[52] This official action was practically equivalent to a dogmatic definition. It seems now that the famous anathemas of St. Cyril, traditionally associated with the Council of Ephesus, were probably not read on that occasion, but rather at the Second Council of Constantinople in 553. The first one reads: "If any one does not profess that Emmanuel is truly God, and that consequently the Holy Virgin is the Mother of God (*Theotokos*), inasmuch as she gave birth in the flesh to the Word of God made flesh . . . , let him be anathema."[53] It is, therefore, an article of our Catholic faith that Mary is really and truly the Mother of God. In 451 the Council of Chalcedon had already inserted the word *Theotokos* in one of its canons.[54] The nature and basis of the Catholic teaching

[52] Sections of the letter are given in DB, 111[a]. The letter, with explicit reference to *Theotokos*, may be found in PG, 77, 43–45.

[53] DB, 113. Cf. Mansi, 9 (Paris-Leipzig, 1909), 327; Carroll, *art. cit.*, 9, Palmer, *op. cit.*, 10.

[54] DB, 148. Cf. P. Galtier, S.J., *Les anathématismes de s. Cyrille et le Concile de Calcedoine*, in RSR, 23 (1933), 45–57.

on this point were authoritatively explained more recently by Pope Pius XI in his encyclical *Lux veritatis* written in 1931 to commemorate the anniversary of the Council of Ephesus.[55]

III. *The Argument from Sacred Scripture.* The Bible nowhere uses the expression "Mother of God." It refers to Mary as "the mother of Jesus" and "the mother of the Lord."[56] However, since Christ is true God, it follows that all texts which refer to Mary as His Mother, are so many proofs of her divine Maternity. Thus, the fulfillment of the prophecy of Isaias was announced by the Archangel Gabriel in these words: "Behold thou shalt conceive in thy womb and shalt bring forth a son, and thou shalt call his name Jesus." And he added: "Therefore, the Holy one who shall be born of thee shall be called the Son of God" (Luke 1:31). We gather the same truth from the following statement of St. Paul:

"When the fullness of time was come, God sent his son, made of a woman" (Galatians 4:4).

IV. *The Teaching of Tradition.* Primitive Christian belief in Mary's divine Maternity is evidenced in the liturgical prayers used by the faithful, particularly the Apostles' Creed wherein they professed faith in "Jesus Christ, His only Son, Our Lord, who was conceived by the Holy Ghost, born of the Virgin Mary." Similarly, the early Fathers of the Church boldly proclaimed the same doctrine, not by employing the term *Theotokos* itself,

[55] AAS, 23 (1931), 493–517.
[56] Cf. LeFrois, *art. cit.*, 102–119.

but by affirming that Christ, who was the Son of God, was truly born of the Virgin Mary. St. Irenaeus of Lyons (d. 202), Tertullian (d. 222/3), Novatian of Rome (d. *c.* 253), St. Cyprian of Carthage (d. 258), and St. Hippolytus of Rome (d. 235) are all witnesses to this dogma.[57] Whether or not Hippolytus was the first to use the word *Theotokos* is disputed.[58] The ancient prayer *Sub tuum praesidium* does address Our Lady under that title, but scholars are not agreed as to the exact date of its original composition. It was written certainly before the close of the fourth century.[59] The first undisputed use of the expression *Theotokos* was made, according to W. J. Burghardt, around the year 319 by Bishop Alexander of Alexandria.[60] The term occurs likewise in St. Ambrose of Milan (d. 397) and St. Vincent of Lerins (d. 450).[61] Of course, after the Council of Ephesus in 431, no disagreement was possible among Catholics on this point.[62]

V. *Theological Explanation of the Catholic Dogma.* The objection of the Nestorians against the term *Theo-*

[57] St. Irenaeus, *Adversus haereses*, 3, 19, 2; PG, 7, 940; Tertullian, *De patientia*, 3; CSEL, 43, 3; Novatian, *De Trinitate*, 9 ff.; PL, 3, 927 ff.; St. Cyprian, *Ad Quirinum testimonia*, 2, 9; CSEL, 3, 73; St. Hippolytus, *Contra Noetum*, 17; PG, 10, 825–828.

[58] Cf. St. Hippolytus, *De benedictionibus Jacob*, 1; TuU, 38, part 1, 13. Cf. Burghardt, *art. cit.*, in *Mariology* (Carol), 1, 134–135; G. Jouassard, *Marie à travers la patristique*, in *Marie* (du Manoir), 1, 86.

[59] Cf. O. Stegmüller, *Sub tuum praesidium: Bemerkungen zur ältesten Uberlieferung*, in ZfkT, 74 (1952), 76–82; Burghardt, *art. cit.*, 132–133.

[60] *Epistola ad Alexandrum Constant.*, 12; PG, 18, 568; Burghardt, *art. cit.*, 135.

[61] St. Ambrose, *De virginibus*, 2, 2, 7; PL, 16, 209; St. Vincent of Lerins, *Commonitorium*, 1, 15; PL, 50, 658.

[62] Cf. M. J. Healy, *The Divine Maternity in the Early Church*, in MS, 6 (1955), 41–62, esp. 53–62.

tokos was based on a false notion of motherhood, and also of the Hypostatic Union.[63] To understand the Catholic dogma, we must have exact ideas concerning both. Motherhood is the relationship established when a woman communicates to her offspring a nature identical to her own, and this by means of a true generation (conception, gestation, birth). The terminus of generation is the whole son, not only the physical body furnished by the mother. Thus, we say that St. Ann is the mother of Mary (i.e., this whole and complete person: Mary), and not only of Mary's body, even though we know that St. Ann did not furnish Mary's soul.

In Christ there are two natures (one divine, one human), and these two natures are inseparably united in *one* Person, namely, the Second Person of the Most Holy Trinity. That most perfect union is called the Hypostatic Union.

Now Mary did not supply Christ with either His divine nature or His divine Person. Both existed from all eternity. She furnished only His human nature. But since that human nature was inseparably united to the divine Person in the very first instant of Christ's conception, we say that Mary conceived and gave birth to a Son who is truly God, and hence she is the Mother of God.

[63] We abstract here from the disputed question of whether or not Nestorius himself held the heretical views traditionally attributed to him. On this whole controversy cf. J. L. Shannon, O.S.A., *Was Nestorius a Nestorian?*, in *MS*, 6 (1955), 120–130; likewise J. Montalverne, O.F.M., *Theodoreti Cyrensis doctrina antiquior de Verbo "inhumanato"* (Rome, 1948), esp. 7–8 and 120–131; and T. Harapin, O.F.M., *De divina Maternitate B. Mariae Virginis*, in *CFS*, 2 (1940), 39–86, esp. 48–68.

The fact that there are two natures in Christ entails a twofold sonship. Because His divine nature was generated from the Father from all eternity, Christ is the true Son of God the Father. Because His human nature was generated from Mary, Christ is the true Son of Mary. However, this twofold sonship does not imply two Sons. Being one undivided Person, Christ the Son of the eternal Father is absolutely identical with Christ the Son of Mary. Hence Mary is truly the Mother of God. By destroying this oneness of Christ's Person, the Nestorians were led to deny Mary's divine Motherhood. By this same token, when the Church defended and defined Mary's divine Motherhood, she was also safeguarding the revealed Catholic doctrine concerning the Hypostatic Union. They necessarily stand or fall together.[64]

VI. *The Objective Dignity of the Divine Maternity.* By objective dignity here we mean the dignity of the motherhood in itself, that is, abstracting from the plenitude of grace which, as a matter of fact, has always accompanied it. By the very fact that she is the Mother of God, Our Lady is raised to a rank high above that of any other creature. Indeed, we may say that she constitutes a category all her own in the hierarchy of creation. This dignity of hers is unquestionably "the greatest after God," as Pope Pius XI states. It may also be referred to as an infinite dignity (in a relative sense) because of her unique relationship with the infinite God. Just as there

[64] Cf. Pohle-Preuss, *op. cit.,* 10–14.

cannot be anything better and greater than God, so there cannot be anything better or greater than His Mother.[65]

Mary's relationship to the Most Blessed Trinity may be summarized as follows. She is related to God the Father by a certain affinity. This is based on the fact that the eternal Father and Mary have a Son who is common to both, although in a different way. She is related to the Second Person of the Holy Trinity (as Man) by consanguinity, inasmuch as the Person of the Logos in His human nature is the terminus of her motherhood. She is related also to the Third Person of the Blessed Trinity, the Holy Ghost, by a certain affinity, because she is the true Mother of Him who, from all eternity, and together with the eternal Father, "spires" the infinite Love which is the Holy Ghost. Mary is properly styled Spouse of the Holy Spirit because it was by the supernatural operation of the latter that she conceived Christ, the Son of God.

In view of the above, theologians generally admit that, while Mary does not belong to the Hypostatic Union (Christ alone does), yet she belongs to the Hypostatic Order, either directly, according to some (Suárez, Saavedra, Cardinal Lépicier), or at least indirectly, according to others.[66] The reason is that it was in her, and through her own generative act, that the Union was accomplished.

[65] *Summa theologica*, I, 25, 6, ad 4. Cf. Carol, *The Nature of the Blessed Virgin's Ontological Mediation*, in MF, 39 (1939), 449–470.
[66] Cf. Roschini, *op. cit.*, 2, part 1, 187–188; Keuppens, *op. cit.*, 24–25; J. Chiodini, *The Nature of the Divine Maternity*, in MS, 6 (1955), 36–40.

Theologians likewise ask the question whether the divine Maternity is a greater dignity than adoptive filiation (through sanctifying grace), and also greater than the priesthood. Actually, since the termini being compared belong to different orders of reality, a comparison in the strict sense seems impossible. Nevertheless, not a few authors are of the opinion that the divine Maternity by far exceeds the dignity conferred by sanctifying grace, "because it is a much greater dignity to be the Mother of God by nature than to be the child of God by adoption."[67] As to the priesthood, it is generally believed that its dignity is far inferior to that of the divine Maternity. The reason lies in the fact that the terminus of Mary's maternal action is a human nature hypostatically united to the Godhead, while the action of the priest during the consecration renders the existing human nature of Christ present in a sacramental status. Admittedly, Our Lady lacks the powers which the priest has of consecrating and absolving from sin; but it remains true that it is a far greater dignity to be the Mother of God than to be God's minister or ambassador.[68]

[67] Thus Roschini, *Summula Mariologiae*, (Rome, 1952), 76. On the related question of the divine Maternity formally sanctifying Our Lady, cf. G. Van Ackeren, S.J., *Does the Divine Maternity Formally Sanctify Mary's Soul?*, in MS, 6 (1955), 63–101.

[68] Cf. W. G. Most, *Is the Priest "Greater" than Mary?*, in Eml, 61 (April, 1955), 155–158.

CHAPTER FOUR

Mary, the Mother of God's Creatures

As INDICATED in the general outline of this book, the first immediate consequence of Mary's divine Maternity is her motherhood with regard to God's intelligent creatures, namely, angels and men. Of God she is the physical Mother; of angels and men she is the spiritual Mother. Strictly speaking, the divine Maternity (taken in the abstract) does not necessarily call for Mary's motherhood of either angels or men. Nevertheless, in the present historical order, that is, presupposing the fall and the Redemption, it is clear that the former is ordained to the latter, inasmuch as God became Man in Mary's womb precisely in order to incorporate His creatures to Himself through the communication of supernatural life. In this sense, Mary's spiritual Maternity may be considered a logical extension, so to say, of her divine Motherhood.

Before discussing the various aspects of this question, we must explain briefly what we understand by the term "mother" when used in this connection. Obviously, when we say that Mary is the Mother of angels and men, we do *not* mean: (a) that she is their Mother in the natural order (as she was the Mother of Christ); (b) that she is their Mother in a purely metaphorical sense (as when we speak of "mother earth" or "mother country"); (c) finally, that she is their Mother in a merely juridical sense (as is the case with human adoption). Our Lady is the Mother of God's children in the supernatural order, in the order of grace, inasmuch as they all have received from her (with and under Christ) the supernatural life which makes them true children of God and members of the Mystical Body of Christ. When and how this was accomplished, we shall see later. Let us now divide the treatment of this question in two different sections or articles dealing with: 1. Mary, the Mother of Angels, and 2. Mary, the Mother of Men.

Article 1

MARY, THE MOTHER OF ANGELS

A woman becomes a mother through the communication of life to her offspring. In the supernatural order this communication of life (which is sanctifying grace) takes place either through generation or through regeneration. The first mode of operation applies to the case of the angels, and to Adam and Eve before the fall. The second applies to the entire human race after the fall. Our thesis is that Our Blessed Lady has a right to be styled Mother of the angels in the true (though analogical) sense of the word, inasmuch as they received all their supernatural life in view of the future merits of Our

Lady, with and under Christ. While this thesis is not fully endorsed by certain groups of theologians (for example, those of the Thomistic School), it would seem to follow with sufficient clearness from the positive data of revelation, namely Sacred Scripture and Tradition, and also to be demanded by good logic. Let us examine the question from this threefold point of view.

I. *The Argument from Sacred Scripture.* Sacred Scripture does not furnish any direct proof to the effect that Our Lady is the spiritual Mother of the angels. Nevertheless, from its teaching concerning the absolute primacy of Christ, we may draw a legitimate conclusion in favor of our doctrine. For example, St. Paul writes to the Colossians that Christ is "the firstborn of every creature: for in him were all things created in heaven and on earth, visible and invisible, whether thrones or dominations or principalities or powers: all things were created by him and in him. And he is before all, and by him all things consist. And he is the head of the body, the Church, who is the beginning, the firstborn from the dead; that in all things he may hold the primacy: Because in him it hath well pleased (the Father) that all fullness should dwell, and through him to reconcile all things unto himself, making peace through the blood of his cross, both as to the things that are on earth and the things that are in heaven" (Colossians 1:15–20).

From the above passage we may argue as follows. In the mind of God from all eternity, Christ is the first of the predestined. Since "that which is first in any genus is also the cause of all that follow,"[69] Christ not only enjoys an absolute primacy over all, but He is likewise the meritorious cause of the supernatural life of all intelligent creatures, including the angels. For this reason St. Paul expressly attributes to Him the reconciliation of all things *in heaven* and on earth. The same grace of Christ which saved men after the fall, prevented the angels from falling.[70] Now since Our Blessed Lady was predestined in one and the same decree with Christ (as we saw above), we conclude that she not only shares His primacy over all creation, but is also the secondary meritorious cause of the grace given to the angels. In this sense she is their spiritual Mother.[71]

II. *The Argument from Tradition.* Early Tradition does not bear explicit witness to this thesis. It is during the Middle Ages that we begin to find clear references to it. Oger of Locedio (fl. 1214) seems to have been the first to use the expression "Mother of Angels."[72] He was followed by pseudo-Albert the Great (end of thirteenth century), St. Antonine of Florence (d. 1459), and Maurice of Villepreux, O.P. (fl. 1512).[73] Gregory Palamas (d. 1360)

---

[69] *Summa Theologica*, III, 1, in corp.

[70] St. Bernard, *Sermo 22, in Cant.*; PL, 183, 880.

[71] Cf. [Ch. Urrutibéhety, O.F.M.], *Marie dans l'école franciscaine* (Lille, 1900), 14–23, 56.

[72] *In lament. B. V. M.*; quoted in H. Marracci, *Polyanthea Mariana* (Cologne, 1727), 388, as the work of St. Bernard. Cf. PL 182, 1139.

[73] St. Antonine, *Summa Theologica*, pars 4, tit. 15, cap. 14 (Verona, 1740), 1003; Maurice of Villepreux, *Nova corona Mariae* (Paris, 1512), *sermo* 3; quoted in Marracci, *op. cit.*, 408.

and Theophane of Nicea (d. 1371) expressly state that
the angels received their grace and glory through Mary.[74]
The thesis may likewise be deduced from the teaching of
many Fathers and early writers who hold that the angels
owe their supernatural life to the foreseen merits of
Christ.[75] Since Our Lady shared Christ's meritorious
causality with regard to all intelligent creatures, she, too,
merited the supernatural life of the angels and, in this
sense, she is their spiritual Mother.

III. *The Argument from Reason.* The unity and harmony of the divine plan seem to demand Our Lady's
spiritual Motherhood with regard to the angels. Indeed,
Christ and Mary are the final cause, the *raison d'être* of
all creation. All inanimate things and all rational beings
(including the angels) were created in view of Christ and
Mary, and for their honor and glory, since that which is
less noble and perfect is always ordained to that which is
more noble and perfect.[76] Hence, whatever good (natural
or supernatural) was ever granted to any creature, including the angels, was granted in view of the foreseen merits
of Christ and His Blessed Mother.[77]

[74] Gregory Palamas, *In dormit. Deiparae*; PG, 151, 473; Theophane
of Nicea, *Sermo in SS. Deiparam*, ed. M. Jugie (1935), 167; ref. taken
from Roschini, *op. cit.*, 2, part 1, 199.
[75] Cf. St. Hilary of Poitiers, *De Trinitate*, 8, 50; PL, 9, 642; St.
Ambrose, *Orat. 8 in S. Theophaniam*; PG, 65, 762. These and many
other references may be found in Roschini, *op. cit.*, 2, part 1, 198, and
in Chrysostome [Urrutibéhety], O.F.M., *Le motif de l'Incarnation
et les principaux thomistes contemporains* (Tours, 1921), 168–202.
[76] *Summa Theologica*, I, 105, 5.
[77] Cf. Roschini, *La Madonna . . .*, 2, 234–237.

Article 2

MARY, THE MOTHER OF MEN

The fact that Mary is the spiritual Mother of all the heavenly spirits, whose nature far surpasses ours, has thrown considerable emphasis on her personal rank and glory. The fact that she is also *our* Mother will undoubtedly heighten the sense of gratitude which we ought to feel toward her. In order to have a fair appreciation of this consoling truth, we shall discuss briefly the following points:

    I. the meaning of the doctrine;
    II. the voice of the magisterium;
    III. the voice of Sacred Scripture;
    IV. the voice of Tradition;
    V. theological explanation of the doctrine;
    VI. its extent.

I. *Meaning of the Doctrine.* Here we must recall summarily what we said above in connection with Mary and the angels. When we state that Mary is the Mother of men we do not mean, of course, that she has given birth to them in the natural, physical order. Again, her maternity of mankind is not simply a figure of speech, or a mere legal fiction. When we style Mary our Mother we mean that she really and truly communicated to us the life of grace which makes us children of God.

II. *The Voice of the Magisterium.* If there is a Marian doctrine (not yet defined) which has been clearly and repeatedly taught by the magisterium, it is the doctrine now under discussion. The first pope to refer to Mary as our Mother ("Mother of grace") was the Franciscan Pope Sixtus IV in his Apostolic Constitution *Cum praecelsa* (February 27, 1477).[78] Not less than twenty-four subsequent popes have declared the same truth, always with increasing clearness and emphasis, particularly since the time of Leo XIII.[79] We shall select but two of the numerous papal texts which could be quoted in this connection. The first is found in St. Pius X's memorable encyclical *Ad diem illum* (February 2, 1904): "Is not Mary the Mother of Christ? She is, therefore, our Mother also. Indeed everyone must believe that Jesus, the Word made flesh, is also the Savior of the human race. Now, as the God-Man, He acquired a body composed like that of other men, but as the Savior of our race, He had a kind of spiritual and mystical body, which is the society of those who believe in Christ. . . . But the Virgin conceived the Eternal Son not only that He might be made man . . . but also . . . that He might be the Savior of men. . . . So, in one and the same bosom of His most chaste Mother, Christ took to Himself human flesh, and at the same time, united to Himself the spiritual body built up of those who are to believe in Him. Consequently, Mary, bearing in her womb the Savior, may be said to have borne also all those whose life was contained

[78] Mansi, 32 (Paris-Leipzig, 1901), 373; critical ed. in Ch. Sericoli, O.F.M., *Immaculata B. M. Virginis Conceptio juxta Xysti IV constitutiones* (Rome, 1945), 153.
[79] Cf. G. W. Shea, *The Teaching of the Magisterium on Mary's Spiritual Maternity*, in MS, 3 (1952), 35–110.

in the life of the Savior. All of us, therefore, . . . have come forth from the womb of Mary as a body united to its head. Hence, in a spiritual and mystical sense, we are called children of Mary, and she is the Mother of us all."[80]

The second text is taken from Pope Pius XII. In his broadcast to the Marian Congress at Ottawa (June 19, 1947), he said: "But when the young maid at Nazareth uttered her *fiat* to the message of the angel, and the Word was made flesh in her womb, she became not only the Mother of God in the physical order of nature, but also, in the supernatural order of grace, she became the Mother of all who, through the Holy Spirit, would be made one under the Headship of her divine Son."[81]

III. *The Voice of Sacred Scripture.* There are a few texts in the Bible which point to the fact that Mary is the spiritual Mother of mankind.[82] For example, the Protoevangelium (Genesis 3:15) studied above, yields the following argument. Mary, "the Woman" of the oracle, is prophesied as sharing most intimately with her divine Son the work of crushing the devil's dominion, which work implies the Redemption of mankind. Now, Christ's Redemption was the concrete manner in which He brought about the regeneration of the human race to the life of grace, lost by sin. Since Mary was Christ's co-

[80] *ASS*, 36 (1904), 452–453.
[81] *AAS*, 39 (1947), 271. Cf. also Shea, *art. cit.*, 98–110.
[82] Cf. E. May, O.F.M.Cap., *The Scriptural Basis for Mary's Spiritual Maternity*, in *MS*, 3 (1952), 111–141.

agent in this process, it follows that she, too, in a subordinate manner, cooperated in our supernatural rebirth,
and hence is our spiritual Mother.

The other classical text is found in the gospel according to St. John (19:26–27): "Jesus, therefore, seeing his
mother and the disciple standing whom he loved, said
to his mother: 'Woman, behold thy son.' Then he said
to the disciple: 'Behold thy mother.' " While not a few
biblical scholars still contend that this passage does not
refer to Mary's spiritual Motherhood of us, the majority
of theologians and Catholic writers insist that it does.
The strongest argument in favor of this latter position is
the unquestionable fact that several popes have interpreted the above passage in that sense. Thus Leo XIII in
his encyclical *Adjutricem populi* (1895) wrote: "Now in
John, according to the constant mind of the Church,
Christ designated the whole human race, particularly
those who were joined with Him by faith."[83] Benedict
XIV, in the bull *Gloriosae Dominae* (1748) seems to
have been the first pope to give this Marian interpretation to the Johannine text.[84] In the light of the above
papal declarations we do not quite understand how it is
possible for so many Catholic scholars to hold that
Christ's words from the cross refer to Mary's spiritual
Motherhood only by accommodation.

IV. *The Voice of Tradition.* The doctrine of Mary's

[83] ASS, 28 (1895–1896), 130. Cf. also ASS, 35 (1902–1903), 627.
[84] *Benedicti XIV opera omnia*, 16 (Prati, 1846), 428.

52   FUNDAMENTALS OF MARIOLOGY

spiritual Motherhood is implicitly contained in the teaching of the ancient Church concerning Mary's role as the Second Eve.[85] St. Epiphanius (d. 403) is the first, so far as we know, to give Our Lady the title of "Mother of the living."[86] With St. Anselm of Canterbury (d. 1109) and Rupert of Deutz (d. 1135) the doctrine received further development,[87] reaching its climax with pseudo-Albert the Great at the end of the thirteenth century.[88] At the present time belief in Mary's spiritual Motherhood is so universally and unquestionably accepted in the Catholic Church, that some authors, like Cardinal Lépicier, are of the opinion that this doctrine is practically an article of our faith.[89]

V. *Theological Explanation of the Doctrine.* Theologically, the spiritual Maternity is closely connected with the doctrine of the Mystical Body and of Mary's intimate share in the Savior's redemptive work. In conceiving Christ, the Head of the Mystical Body, Mary conceived all of us, because we are members of that Body. Mary gave physical life to the Head (Christ) so that the

[85] Cf. W. R. O'Connor, *The Spiritual Maternity of Our Lady in Tradition,* in MS, 3 (1952), 142–147.

[86] *Adversus haereses,* 3, 2; PG, 42, 728–729.

[87] St. Anselm, *Oratio* 52; PL, 158, 957; Rupert of Deutz, *Commentarius in Joannem,* 13; PL, 169, 789–790. For further testimonies of this period, cf. I. Ruidor, S.J., *María Mediadora y Madre del Cristo Místico en los escritores eclesiásticos de la primera mitad del siglo XII,* in EE, 25 (1951), 181–218.

[88] *Mariale,* 2. 150; in B. *Alberti Magni . . . opera omnia,* ed. A. Borgnet, 37 (Paris, 1898), 219.

[89] A. H. M. Lépicier, O.S.M., *Tractatus de Beatissima Virgine Maria Matre Dei,* 5th ed. (Rome, 1926). 465.

members might receive their spiritual life from Him.[90] Hence Mary became our Mother already at the time of the Annunciation, but only inchoatively and imperfectly. Her Motherhood of us culminated and was perfected on Calvary, because it was there that she actually brought about the spiritual regeneration of the human race (with and under Christ), by being a co-agent in Christ's Redemption. It is for this reason that, in the present order of things, the concept of spiritual Motherhood and the concept of Coredemption are inseparable and, in some aspects, actually coincide.[91]

Although the human race, as a whole, was reborn to the life of grace on Calvary through the joint operation of Christ and Mary, yet, as individuals, we become incorporated into the Body of Christ, i.e., we are actually born to the supernatural life, at the time of Baptism. It is then that the supernatural life merited for us by Christ and Mary is actually infused into our souls. But Our Lady's maternal action does not stop there. She continues nourishing and developing that life in our souls by means of the many actual graces which she obtains for us. This latter activity of Mary in our regard does not constitute her Motherhood of us; it is rather a sequel of her Mother-

[90] Cf. Basilio de San Pablo, C.P., *La divina maternidad es intrínsecamente sosteriológica*, in *EM*, 8 (1949), 257–297. For the opposite view, cf. Crisóstomo de Pamplona, O.F.M.Cap., *De divina Maternitate ad Corredemptionem et Maternitatem spiritualem relata*, in *ASC*, 2, 118–132.

[91] Cf. W. Sebastian, O.F.M., *The Nature of Mary's Spiritual Maternity*, in *MS*, 3 (1952), 14–34, esp. 30–34.

hood, or if you will, one of the ways in which she exercises her maternal office.[92]

VI. *Extent of Mary's Spiritual Motherhood.* Mary's spiritual Maternity extends to all those who come under the Headship of Christ. That includes all rational creatures, angels and men, although in a different manner according to the degree in which they share the life of grace merited by Christ. Hence Mary is in no way the Mother of the damned, because they are definitively cut off from participation in the supernatural life. *Potentially,* she is the Mother of all infidels, because they are destined to be united with Christ through faith and charity. *Actually,* though imperfectly, she is the Mother of all sinners who are still united with Christ by faith; perfectly, she is the Mother of all the just who live the life of grace.

[92] J. M. Bover, S.J., *Mediación de Madre, o la Mediación universal como actuación de la Maternidad de María* (Covadonga, 1927).

Mary's Universal Mediation

THE second logical corollary of Our Lady's sublime mission as Mother of God is her universal Mediation. This mediatorial office may be considered also as an immediate consequence of Mary's role as spiritual Mother of the Mystical Body, but only in the sense that this Motherhood had a logical priority in the mind of God. In the order of execution, however, the Mediation (at least some aspects of it) precedes the spiritual Motherhood, inasmuch as the former is used by God as a means to bring about the latter. In point of fact, some phases of the Mediation seem to coincide with some phases of the spiritual Motherhood. In a sense, therefore, it is correct to say that Mary is our spiritual Mother *because* she is our Mediatrix, and also that she is our Mediatrix *because* she is our spiritual Mother.[93]

The function of a "mediator" is to intervene between two persons or groups of persons in order to bring them together. The nature of his role will depend largely on the existing circumstances. At times he will interpose his services simply to facilitate an exchange of favors between the parties. In most cases, however, the persons

[93] Here we modify an opinion previously held against N. García Garcés in our article *Adnotationes in opus "Mater Corredemptrix" a Patre N. Garcia conscriptum*, in Mm, 8 (1946), 277–283; cf. 278, footnote 1.

for whom he mediates happen to be at variance and, therefore, his function is usually to reconcile the extremes. This is the notion of mediation in general.

When applied to Our Blessed Lady the term "Mediatrix" designates a twofold[94] function: first, reconciling mankind with God through her cooperation in the redemptive work of Christ while she was still on earth; second, making available to each individual soul the graces which were earned by Christ and by herself through the work of Redemption. The first phase of her Mediation was accomplished on Calvary; the second is being constantly carried out and will continue until the end of the world. In virtue of the first function Mary is called "Coredemptrix"; in virtue of the second, "Dispenser of all graces." We shall now treat these aspects of that mediatorial office in two separate articles.

Article 1

MARY, COREDEMPTRIX OF MANKIND

Our Blessed Lady has been hailed as "Coredemptrix" of the human race at least since the 15th century.[95] This title, which has become quite common among Catholic writers, is frequently employed also by the Catholic

---

[94] We abstract here and now from what is called *ontological* Mediation. Cf. Carol, *The Theological Concept of Mediation and Coredemption,* in ETL, 14 (1937), 642–650.

[95] Cf. R. Laurentin, *Le titre de Corédemptrice; étude historique,* in Mm, 13 (1951), 396–452.

hierarchy, and is found even in some papal documents.[96] Hence its legitimacy is now beyond question. But more important than the word "Coredemptrix" itself, is the doctrine conveyed by that word. It is here that we encounter a good deal of discussion and conflicting opinions on the part of Catholic theologians. The treatment of this complex question may be conveniently divided into the following sections:

    I. the meaning of Redemption and Coredemption;

    II. various opinions concerning Mary's Coredemption;

    III. the teaching of the magisterium;

    IV. the argument from Sacred Scripture;

    V. the teaching of Tradition;

    VI. objections against the doctrine.

I. *The Meaning of Redemption and Coredemption.* In Catholic theology the term "Redemption" designates the sum total of meritorious and satisfactory acts performed by Christ while on earth, offered to the eternal Father in and through the sacrifice of the cross, in virtue of which the eternal Father was moved (humanly speaking) to reinstate the human race into His former friendship.

Accordingly, when we say that Our Lady is the "Coredemptrix" of mankind we mean that, together with Christ (although subordinately to Him and in virtue of His power) she atoned or satisfied for our sins, merited

[96] Cf. Carol, *The Holy See and the Title of "Coredemptrix,"* in HPR, 37 (1937), 746–748; Id., *Episcoporum doctrina de Beata Virgine Corredemptrice,* in Mm, 10 (1948), 210–258.

every grace necessary for salvation, and offered her divine Son on Calvary to appease the wrath of God, and that, as a result of this, God was pleased to cancel our debt and receive us into His former friendship. This coredemptive role of Mary actually began when she, out of her own free will, made possible the coming of the Redeemer into the world by accepting to become His Mother. She did this realizing that her Motherhood of the Redeemer implied her close association with her Son in His saving mission. This role of hers had its culmination on Calvary where, together with Christ, she interposed the meritorious and satisfactory value of her compassion to help reconcile the human race with God. By the fact that Mary brought the Redeemer into the world, in the manner just explained, she cooperated *mediately* or remotely in the work of our Redemption. By the fact that she joined her merits and satisfactions with those of the Savior and for the same purpose, she cooperated *immediately* or proximately in the Redemption.

II. *Various Opinions Concerning Mary's Coredemption.* Non-Catholics, in general, are of the opinion that Our Lady can in no way be styled Coredemptrix. For them, she was merely the physical and material instrument chosen by God to send us our only Redeemer. On the contrary, Catholics are all in agreement that Mary cooperated in Christ's redemptive work not only physically and materially, but also formally, inasmuch as she knowingly and willingly accepted to become the Mother of the Redeemer as such. But they disagree when they

attempt to determine further the nature and extent of
that cooperation. Some theologians are of the opinion
that Mary's cooperation, while formal, was nevertheless
only remote or mediate.[97] At the present time, however,
the vast majority of authors hold that her cooperation
was also proximate and immediate, in the sense explained
above.[98]

III. *The Teaching of the Magisterium.* The magisterium has not as yet settled the theological controversy
concerning Mary's Coredemption. However, there are
not a few passages in papal documents which reveal to
us the mind of the Church on this matter. We shall refer
here to only a few statements made by recent popes.[99]

Benedict XV in his Apostolic Letter *Inter sodalicia*
(March 22, 1918) wrote as follows: "To such extent did
she (Mary) suffer and almost die with her suffering and
dying Son, and to such extent did she surrender her
maternal rights over her Son for man's salvation, and
immolated Him, insofar as she could, in order to appease

[97] For example, H. Lennerz, S.J., *De cooperatione B. Virginis in ipso
opere redemptionis,* in *Gr,* 28 (1947), 576–597; 29 (1948), 118–141;
G. D. Smith, *Mary's Part in our Redemption,* 2nd ed. (New York,
1954), 92–99.
[98] See the lengthy list of authors given in our work *De Corredemptione* . . . (Vatican City, 1950), 49–52.
[99] For the teaching of the bishops, cf. Carol, *op. cit.,* 539–619. It
may be of interest to recall here that on November 26, 1951, a formal
petition was submitted to the Holy See by His Eminence, Emmanuel
Cardinal Arteaga y Betancourt, Archbishop of Havana, and the entire
Cuban hierarchy, urging the dogmatic definition of Our Lady's Coredemption. Although the text of the document has not been made
public, we happen to know that the signatories requested the Pope to
define this doctrine *in exactly the same sense* defended in this chapter.
The fact is significant because it represents the first time in history that a
step of this nature is taken by the collective episcopate of any nation.

the justice of God, that *we may rightly say that she re-deemed the human race together with Christ.*"[100]

In the radio broadcast to the world at the solemn closing of the Jubilee Year which commemorated the Redemption of mankind (April 29, 1935), Pope Pius XI addressed Our Lady in these words: "O Mother of piety and mercy who, when thy most beloved Son was accomplishing the Redemption of the human race on the altar of the cross, didst stand there both suffering with Him and *as a Coredemptrix*; preserve in us, we beseech thee, and increase day by day, the precious fruit of His Redemption *and* of thy compassion."[101] This same pope called Our Lady "Coredemptrix" on at least five other occasions.[102]

A statement somewhat similar to the one made by Benedict XV is found also in the encyclical *Mystici Corporis* (June 29, 1943) of Pius XII.[103] In his broadcast to the faithful gathered in Fátima in 1946, this same pope stated that just as Mary had been associated with Christ in the work of man's Redemption, as Mother and cooperatrix, so likewise now she is perpetually associated with Him in the distribution of all the graces which flow from that Redemption.[104] More recently, in his encyclical

[100] In AAS, 10 (1918), 182. Cf. Carol, *The Problem of Our Lady's Coredemption*, in AER, 123 (July, 1950), 32–51, esp. 47–48.

[101] Cf. OssR, April 29–30, 1935, 1.

[102] Cf. Roschini, *La Madonna nel pensiero e nell'insegnamento di Pio XI*, in Mm, 1 (1939), 131 144, 148–149, 151, 164.

[103] AAS, 35 (1943), 247–248.

[104] AAS, 38 (1946), 266. Cf. Carol, *Mary's Coredemption in the Teaching of Pope Pius XII*, in AER, 121 (November, 1949), 353–361.

Ad coeli Reginam (October 11, 1954), the Holy Father again distinguishes Our Lady's cooperation in the Redemption as such, from her role as Mother of the Savior and dispenser of all heavenly graces.[105]

IV. *The Argument from Sacred Scripture.* The Bible nowhere calls Mary "Coredemptrix" of the human race, either expressly or equivalently. Nevertheless, there are some passages in the Sacred Book in which this doctrine is implied.[106] The most important of these is the Protoevangelium (Genesis 3:15). Here we read that, after the fall of our first parents, Almighty God addressed their tempter (the devil under the appearance of a serpent) with these words: "I will put enmities between thee and the woman, between thy seed and her seed. He (the woman's seed) shall crush thy head and thou shalt lie in wait for his heel." The crushing of the serpent's head is, of course, a figure of speech used here to describe the work of Redemption which will utterly destroy the devil's power over men.[107] As we have endeavored to show elsewhere, the seed of the woman is Christ, as an individual, and the woman mentioned in the text designates Our Blessed Lady.[108] Since, according to the magisterium, Mary is here portrayed as intimately sharing Christ's

[105] AAS, 46 (1954), 633–637; in the English translation published by the Vatican (1954), 10–13. Cf. the excellent study by W. G. Most, *De Corredemptione et regalitate in epistola encyclica "Ad coeli Reginam,"* in *Mm,* 17 (1955), 354–368.

[106] Cf. R. Rábanos, C.M., *La Corredención de María en la Sagrada Escritura,* in *EM,* 2 (1943), 9–59.

[107] Cf. above, footnote 40.

[108] Cf. above, Ch. 2, art. 1.

identical victory over Satan, it follows that she is herein foreshadowed as the world's Coredemptrix.[109]

Again, in the New Testament (Luke 1:26–38) we are told how the Angel Gabriel was sent by God to ask Mary's consent to become the Mother of the Redeemer. Mary answered: "Behold the handmaid of the Lord; be it done unto me according to thy word." In a very true sense, then, God made the Redemption of the world dependent upon Mary's consent; and she gave it knowingly and willingly. This consent was undoubtedly ratified on Calvary when she stood at the foot of the cross suffering with her Son (Luke 2:35) and indeed for the selfsame purpose, namely the reconciliation of God and man.[110]

V. *The Teaching of Tradition*. The germ idea of our present-day teaching concerning Mary's Coredemption was already contained in the ancient doctrine portraying her in the role of a New and Second Eve. Beginning with St. Justin Martyr (d. 163) and particularly St. Irenaeus (d. 202), not a few of the early Fathers and Christian writers establish a striking contrast between Mary and Eve. The essence of the antithesis lies in this, that just as Eve cooperated with Adam in the sin that doomed the whole race, so Mary has cooperated with Christ, the second Adam, in bringing about the rehabilitation of mankind lost by that sin; just as Eve, through

[109] Pius XII *Munificientissimus Deus*, in AAS, 42 (1950), 769.
[110] Cf. Carol, *Our Lady's Coredemption*, in *Mariology* (Carol), 2, Ch. 10; likewise C. Boyer, S.J., *Thoughts on Mary's Coredemption*, in AER, 122 (June, 1950), 401–415.

her disobedience, had become the cause of death and damnation to her race, so Mary, through her acquiescence to God's will at the time of the Annunciation, had become the cause of life and salvation to mankind.[111] Explicitly, then, the patristic texts emphasizing this antithetical parallelism bear exclusively on Our Lady's *mediate* cooperation in the world's Redemption, in the sense explained above. Implicitly, however, they may be said to contain later developments of the doctrine. In other words, the theologians of subsequent centuries simply elaborated and carried to its ultimate conclusions what had been preached in the Church from the remotest times only in embryonic fashion. Thus, in the 12th century, and particularly under the influence of Arnold of Chartres (d. 1160), we begin to find frequent and specific allusions to the redemptive character of Our Lady's compassion and her oblation on Calvary.[112] By the end of the 17th century, a large number of theologians and Catholic writers were already teaching the doctrine of Mary's Coredemption in exactly the same sense as we do today.[113]

[111] Cf. Burghardt, *art. cit.*, 110–117; also the various articles in BSFEM, 12 (1954).
[112] Arnold of Chartres, *De septem verbis Domini in cruce; PL*, 189, 1694; id., *De laudibus B. M. Virginis; PL*, 189, 1726–1727. Cf. A. Luis, C.SS.R., *Evolutio historica doctrinae de compassione B. Mariae Virginis*, in *Mm*, 5 (1943), 280–282; Carol, *op. cit.*, 156–198; L. Riley, *Historical Conspectus of the Doctrine of Mary's Coredemption*, in *MS*, 2 (1951), 27–106, esp. 49–56.
[113] Cf. Carol, *Our Lady's Part in the Redemption according to Seventeenth Century Writers*, in *FS*, 24 (1943), 3–20; 143–158.

VI. *Objections Against Mary's Coredemption.* The main objections raised by the adversaries of Our Lady's Coredemption may be reduced to the following three:

A. According to Sacred Scripture (I Timothy 2:5) and the constant teaching of the Church, Christ alone is our Mediator and Redeemer; He alone wrought our salvation.

Answer: We have seen above that these same sources point to Our Blessed Lady as Christ's associate in the Redemption. Therefore, when they state that Christ alone is our Redeemer, they are obviously referring to the primary, universal and self-sufficient causality of Christ in the redemptive process. This does not exclude Mary's secondary and completely subordinate cooperation which drew all its efficacy from the superabundant merits of her divine Son.

B. Mary herself was redeemed by Christ. How could she, at one and the same time, receive the *effect* of the Redemption and be the *cause* of it?

Answer: Mary cooperated to redeem others, not herself. Christ redeemed Mary first with a preservative Redemption, and then, together with her, He redeemed all others with a liberative Redemption. This does not, of course, correspond to two distinct Redemptions, but rather to a *twofold* intention on the part of Christ. This twofold intention, in turn, produced a twofold effect: one affecting Mary alone, and the other (with the cooperation of Mary) affecting the rest of mankind. Once Mary was redeemed by Christ (with a logical priority), she was able to cooperate with Him in the Redemption of others.

C. The value of Christ's merits and satisfactions was infinite. How can that value be enhanced by the merits and satisfactions of Our Blessed Lady?

Answer: Our Lady's cooperation did not and could not enhance the value of Christ's redemptive acts. However, God was pleased to accept the former together with the latter merely as constituting a new title for our Redemption. Adam, too, was more than sufficient to ruin the human race with his sin; yet he did not do it alone; he had the effective, though secondary, cooperation of Eve. Since the Redemption was to be a counterpart of the original fall, it was fitting that the Second Eve (Mary) should be a close partner of the Second Adam (Christ) throughout the process of this spiritual rehabilitation. Surely, God could have arranged things otherwise; but He chose to arrange them that way.[114]

Article 2

MARY, DISPENSER OF ALL GRACES

The second phase of Our Lady's universal Mediation refers to her role as Dispenser of all graces. If Mary not only gave us the person of the Redeemer, but also cooperated with Him in His redemptive work (through which all graces were merited or acquired), it stands to

---

[114] A fuller answer to these and several other objections may be found in our article appearing in *Mariology* (Carol), 2, Ch. 10.

reason that she should have a certain right to cooperate with Him in the dispensation or distribution of those same graces to the members of His Mystical Body. In this connection we shall touch upon the following points:

I. the meaning of this Marian prerogative;

II. adversaries of the doctrine;

III. the voice of the magisterium;

IV. the argument from Sacred Scripture;

V. the teaching of Tradition;

VI. objection against the doctrine.

I. *Meaning of this Marian Prerogative.* When we say that Our Lady is the Dispenser of all graces we mean that all favors granted by God to all men are granted in view and because of Mary's intercession. We say *all* favors and graces, without exception, that is: habitual grace, the infused virtues (theological and moral), the gifts of the Holy Ghost, all actual graces, and finally all favors of the natural order insofar as they may help us attain eternal life. We say, *all* men, without exception, regardless of any circumstances of time or space. Those living after the Redemption was accomplished receive all graces through Mary acting as a secondary efficient (moral) cause.[115] Those living before that time, received their graces through Mary acting as a final cause, that is

---

[115] A few authors attribute to Our Lady a *physical* instrumental causality in the dispensation of graces. In our humble opinion, this theory is foreign to the teaching of the magisterium and Catholic tradition; hence, it ought to be rejected. Even some of its more ardent advocates candidly admit that they have no solid arguments to prove it. Cf. R. Garrigou-Lagrange, O.P., *The Mother of the Saviour and our Interior Life* (St. Louis, Mo., 1949), 237. On the whole controversy cf. Roschini, *Mariologia*, 2, part 1, 413–420. Not one of the so-called

to say, they received grace in view of the future merits of Our Lady. The Catholic doctrine on this point does not mean that we must ask for God's graces in Mary's name; but it does mean that, whether we mention her name or not, we get them through her intercession.

II. *Adversaries of the Doctrine.* Protestants and, of course, other non-Catholics in general, deny that Mary is the dispenser of all graces. Among Catholics, the doctrine was rejected, as at least lacking solid foundation, by Theophilus Raynaud, S.J., and Adam Widenfeld, in the 17th century, by L. Muratori, in the 18th century, and by J. Ude, J. Rivière and P. Poschmann in our own times. They admit that Mary may be styled "channel" of all graces only in a broad sense, namely, insofar as she gave birth to Christ who is the source of all grace.[116]

III. *The Voice of the Magisterium.* The doctrine that Mary is the Dispenser of all graces has the full support of the magisterium, particularly of recent Pontiffs. Pope Leo XIII in his encyclical *Octobri mense* (September 22, 1891) wrote as follows: "It may be affirmed truly and in all precision that out of the immense treasure of grace brought to us by Christ . . . absolutely nothing is com-

---

"arguments" given by Roschini in favor of this theory would be considered serious in any other theological tract.

[116] Cf. Th. Raynaud, *Diptycha Mariana*, 10, 14; *opera omnia*, 7 (Lyons, 1665), 224; A. Widenfeld, *Wholesome Advices from the Blessed Virgin to her Indiscreet Worshippers*, tr. J. Taylor (London, 1687), p. 8; L. Muratori, *Della regolata devozione dei cristiani*, Ch. 22; in *Opere del preposto L. A. Muratori . . .* , 6 (Arezzo, 1768), 199–200; J. Ude, *Ist Maria die Mittlerin aller Gnaden? Eine dogmatisch-kritische Untersuchung* (Bressanone, 1928), *passim*, esp. 153; P. Poschmann, in *ThR*, 27 (1928), n. 7, col. 261–265.

municated to us except through Mary."[117] Pope Benedict
XV in his Apostolic Letter *Inter sodalicia* (March 22,
1918), after stating that Mary had redeemed the world
together with Christ, immediately adds: "It is for this
reason that all the graces contained in the treasury of the
Redemption are given to us through the hands of this
same sorrowful Virgin."[118] Similar statements are found
in Pius XI's encyclical *Miserentissimus Redemptor* (May
6, 1928),[119] and also in Pius XII's broadcast to the faithful gathered in Fátima in 1946. Here the Holy Father
points out that just as Our Lady had been associated with
the Savior in the work of man's Redemption, so likewise
now she is perpetually associated with Him in the distribution of all the graces which flow from that Redemption.[120] It should be mentioned under this same heading
that a liturgical feast honoring Mary as Mediatrix of all
graces is celebrated in numerous dioceses of the world on
May 31 of each year. The permission to do so was
originally granted by Pope Benedict XV on January 12,
1921, at the request of Cardinal Mercier, Archbishop of
Malines in Belgium.[121]

IV. *The Voice of Sacred Scripture.* In the Protoevan-

[117] *AAS*, 24 (1891), 195–196. For many other papal texts, cf. A.
Robichaud, S.M., *Mary, Dispensatrix of all Graces*, in *Mariology*
(Carol), 2, Ch. 11.
[118] *AAS*, 10 (1918), 182.
[119] *AAS*, 20 (1928), 178.
[120] *AAS*, 38 (1946), 266.
[121] On the office of this liturgical feast, cf. the interesting observations of J. Lebon, *A propos des textes liturgiques de la fête de Marie
Médiatrice*, in *Mm*, 14 (1952), 122–128.

gelium (Genesis 3:15) Our Lady is shown as intimately associated with Christ in the whole process of Redemption or man's reconciliation with God. Since the actual dispensation of graces is but an aspect of that whole process, it follows (although not with strict necessity) that Mary should have her share in it. Significantly, the New Testament seems to attribute to Mary both the sanctification of John the Baptist in the womb of his mother (Luke 1:41) and the miracle wrought by Christ at the wedding feast of Cana (John 2:1–11). However, these and other New Testament passages are only indications, not proofs.[122]

V. *The Teaching of Tradition.* We possess no explicit testimonies from the ancient Fathers bearing on Mary's prerogative as Dispenser of every single grace. However, as in the case of the Coredemption, and much in the same way, this doctrine may be said to be *implied* in the teaching of the early Church concerning Mary's role as the Second Eve. From the 8th century on, the texts become more explicit. Thus St. Germain of Constantinople (d. 733) addresses the Blessed Virgin: "O most holy One, no one obtains salvation except through thee. . . . There is no one to whom the gift of grace is given, except through thee."[123] A sermon of St. Bernard (d. 1153) on Mary's Nativity has a passage which has become classical in Marian literature: "Such is the will

---

[122] Cf. J. Bittremieux, *De Mediatione universali B. Mariae Virginis quoad gratias* (Bruges, 1926), 180–183.

[123] *Orat. 2 in dormit. Deiparae;* PG, 98, 350.

of God, that we should obtain everything through Mary."[124] The famous *Mariale* long attributed to St. Albert the Great calls Our Lady "aqueduct" inasmuch as all heavenly gifts flow to the human race through her.[125] This and many similar metaphorical expressions became very frequent in the Middle Ages.[126] St. Bernardine of Sienna (d. 1444) has a passage of incomparable clearness: "I do not hesitate to affirm that this same Virgin has a certain jurisdiction over the torrent of all graces . . . ; therefore, all gifts, virtues and graces of the same Holy Spirit are administered through her own hands to whom she wishes, when she wishes, in the manner she wishes, and as much as she wishes."[127]

When the learned Muratori denied this doctrine in the 18th century, St. Alphonsus Liguori (d. 1787) became the leading and most articulate champion of the Catholic teaching on this point.[128] In the 20th century those who have contributed most to the theological clarification of the thesis have been the Spanish Jesuit J. M. Bover, and the Louvain Professor J. Bittremieux.[129] At the present

---

[124] St. Bernard, *In nativ. B. M. V.*; PL, 183, 441. For further testimonies of this important period, cf. I. Ruidor, S.J., *La Mediación de María en la distribución de las gracias según los escritores eclesiásticos de la primera mitad del siglo XII*, in EM, 12 (1952), 301–318.

[125] *Mariale*, p. 164; in *B. Alberti Magni . . . opera omnia*, 37, 241.

[126] Cf. J. M. Bover, S.J., *De universali B. Mariae V. mediatione metaphorica testimonia*, in Mm, 3 (1941), 201–237.

[127] *Sermo de gratia et gloria B. Virginis*, cap. 8; *opera omnia*, 2 (Quaracchi, 1950), 379.

[128] *The Glories of Mary*, ed. E. Grimm (Brooklyn, N.Y., 1931), 152–175; 684–696.

[129] On Bittremieux's writings, cf. J. Coppens, *L'enseignement et l'oeuvre théologique de M. le Chanoine J. Bittremieux*, in ETL, 23 (1947), 367–377. On Bover's publications, cf. the appendix to his own

time, the doctrine is considered by not a few theologians as proximately definable.[130]

VI. *Objection Against the Doctrine.* The sacraments infallibly and automatically produce sanctifying grace in the souls of those who receive them, provided they have the proper dispositions, and the required matter and form have been duly used by the proper minister. If this is so, there are cases in which graces are given to us independently of Mary's intervention. In other words, Mary is not the Dispenser of absolutely *all* graces.

Answer: While Our Blessed Lady does not produce directly and physically the sanctifying grace given to us through the Sacraments, nevertheless, she intervenes in that production in a twofold manner. First, *remotely*, inasmuch as that sacramental grace was merited by her (together with Christ) as Coredemptrix while she was on earth. Secondly, *proximately* (although indirectly), inasmuch as the very desire to receive the Sacraments, and the proper dispositions to do so worthily are the effect of actual graces which are granted to the recipient in each case through the intercession of Our Blessed Lady.[130a]

---

work *María Mediadora universal, o Soteriología Mariana* (Madrid, 1946), 522–532.

[130] Cf. E. Druwé, S.J., *La Médiation universelle de Marie,* in *Maria* (du Manoir), 1, 564–566.

[130a] Cf. the somewhat different explanation offered by B. Piault in his interesting article *De la médiation de la Vierge Marie,* in NRT, 75 (December, 1953), 1020–1038.

CHAPTER SIX

Mary's Universal Queenship

THE third logical consequence of Mary's unique mission is her role as universal Queen. Much attention has been devoted to this thesis in recent years, particularly in view of the repeated declarations of the magisterium. In our presentation of the doctrine we shall endeavor to avoid the two extremes sometimes encountered in this connection, namely, exaggerations *per excessum*, and exaggerations *per defectum*. Our safest guide in the matter will be the magisterium itself. The treatment of this thesis may be conveniently divided into the following sections:

I. explanation of the terms "king" and "queen" in general;

II. the meaning of "queenship" as applied to Mary;

III. the teaching of the magisterium;

IV. the biblical basis of the doctrine;

V. the voice of Tradition;

VI. the extent and nature of Mary's Queenship.

I. *Explanation of the Terms "King" and "Queen" in General.* The words "king" and "queen" are not necessarily synonyms differing only in gender. In most cases, according to the usage universally accepted, they imply functions which are formally different. Since queenship is predicated only analogically of Mary and of earthly queens, and since the office of a queen is related to that of the king, we will first describe the latter in order better to understand the former, and then project these concepts on the specific case of Our Blessed Lady.[131]

A. *Meaning of the word "King."*

(1) In a purely *metaphorical* sense the word "king" connotes simply a certain primacy, prominence or excellence with reference to others of the same genus. In this sense the lion is often called the king of animals; Demosthenes the king of orators, and so forth.

(2) In the *proper* sense a "king" is the man who, on his own authority, rules the members of an organized society and leads them to their common end, exercising his supreme dominion by means of the threefold power: legislative, judicial and coercive.

B. *Meaning of the word "Queen."*

(1) In a purely *metaphorical* sense the word "queen" connotes only a certain primacy, prominence or excellence with reference to others. Thus theology is called the queen of sciences; charity the queen of virtues, and so on.

(2) In the *proper-absolute* sense a queen is a woman who, on her own authority, rules the members of an organized society and leads them to their common end. A queen in this sense exercises her supreme dominion over

---

[131] On this whole chapter, cf. the 4th volume of *Marian Studies* (1953) and the abundant literature indicated therein.

her subjects by means of the threefold power: legislative, judicial, and coercive. Example: the present Queen of Holland.

(3) In the *proper-relative* sense a queen is a woman who shares the dignity and office of a king only in her capacity as the king's mother or as the king's consort. Examples: the Queen-Mother of Denmark, the Queen-Consort of Sweden.

II. *The Meaning of "Queenship" When Applied to Mary.*

A. That Our Blessed Lady may be styled queen in a *metaphorical* sense is obvious. Because of her unsurpassed sanctity and her unique connection with the Hypostatic Order, she automatically holds the highest possible rank, primacy and dignity in God's creation.

B. On the other hand, Mary is not queen in the *proper-absolute* sense of that word. The reason is that Mary is not a "female king," a king of the feminine sex, such as the Queen of Holland or the present Queen of England. Her authority over the subjects of her kingdom is not supreme and independent, but altogether subordinate to that of her Son, the only Supreme Ruler.

C. However, Our Blessed Lady is rightly styled queen in the *proper-relative* sense of that word. She has a right to that title both as Mother of the King (Christ), and as His intimate consort in His mission of leading the members of that kingdom to their common end. Like earthly queens in their own sphere, Mary rules her spiritual subjects mostly through the efficacy of her influence over the heart of the King (insinuations, suggestions, powerful intercession on behalf of the subjects).[132] But this is not all.

D. The term "queenship," when applied to Mary, designates a reality far surpassing the queenly power just described. Mary's Queenship is utterly unique; it is altogether peculiar and proper to *this* Queen. This becomes evident when we consider the specific manner in which she acquired her dominion, and the unique manner in which she exercises her royal powers.

1. Our Blessed Lady acquired her dominion over her subjects, not only by being the Mother of the King and His associate or consort in His mission of leading the members of His kingdom to their common end, but also by the fact that she formally and actively cooperated with the King in the work of Redemption. It was precisely through the Redemption that Christ and Mary recaptured or conquered their kingdom from the unjust possession of Satan. Just as Christ is King because of the Hypostatic Union *and* the added title of conquest (i.e., as Redeemer), so Mary is Queen because of her divine Motherhood and her prerogative as Coredemptrix. In other words, she is Queen by divine relationship and by right of conquest.

2. As to the exercise of her Queenship, it may be said that Our Lady participates in the legislative power of her Son in a unique way. Here we must bear in mind

---

[132] Cf. A. Luis, C.SS.R., *Prerogativas que implica la realeza de María*, in *EM*, 1 (1942), 169–225, esp. 193–196.

that, in the supernatural kingdom of Christ, the law is primarily grace itself, and only secondarily the precepts of the Gospel. It is grace that prompts the subjects of this kingdom to conform to the Ruler's will; it is mainly by grace that they are led to their common end and welfare.[133] Since Our Lady has a certain jurisdiction over the treasury of grace, and since she is the dispenser of all grace, it follows that she shares Christ's legislative power. As to whether or not she shares also the judicial and executive powers, theologians have expressed different opinions. Some, like C. Dillenschneider, say that she does not; others, like G. M. Roschini, believe that she shares them indirectly, through her consent and her prayers.[134]

III. *The Teaching of the Magisterium.* Our Blessed Lady has been openly proclaimed "Queen" by at least fourteen popes between Gregory II (715-731) and Pius XII.[135] The classical text is found in the address of Pius XII to the faithful gathered in Fátima in 1946. His words are clear and categorical: "He, the Son of God, reflects on His heavenly Mother the glory, the majesty, and the dominion of His kingship; for, having been associated with the King of Martyrs in the ineffable work of human Redemption as Mother and cooperatrix, she remains forever associated with Him, with an almost unlimited

---

[133] *Summa Theologica*, I–II, 106, 1, in corp.

[134] C. Dillenschneider, C.SS.R., *Souveraineté de Marie*, in *Compte rendu du Congrès Marial de Boulogne s/M* (Paris, 1938), 140; Roschini, *Mariologia*, 2, part 1, 426.

[135] Cf. E. Carroll, O.Carm., *Our Lady's Queenship in the Magisterium of the Church*, in MS, 4 (1953), 29–81.

power, in the dispensation of graces which flow from the Redemption. Jesus is King throughout all eternity by nature and by right of conquest; through Him, with Him, and subordinate to Him, Mary is Queen by grace, by divine relationship, by right of conquest, and by singular election. And her kingdom is as vast as that of her Son and God, since nothing is excluded from her dominion."[136] These ideas were repeated, in a more elaborate manner, in his recent encyclical *Ad coeli Reginam.*[137] The Sacred Liturgy, too, both in the East and in the West, loudly and frequently proclaims Mary's universal Queenship.[138] The recently established feast in honor of this Marian prerogative is a significant indication of the mind of the Church on this point. The feast is to be observed universally on May 31 of each year.[139]

IV. *The Biblical Basis for Mary's Queenship.* The most important biblical passage in support of Mary's Queenship, understood in the proper sense, is the well-known Protoevangelium (Genesis 3:15). It is here that Our Lady is formally (though implicitly) introduced as Christ's intimate associate in the work of man's Redemption. Since it was precisely the Redemption that gave Christ the title of King by right of conquest, it follows that Mary, too, in her capacity as Coredemptrix, shares Christ's Kingship by right of conquest.[140]

[136] AAS, 38 (1946), 266.
[137] AAS, 46 (1954), 625–640.
[138] Cf. K. B. Moore, O.Carm., *The Queenship of the Blessed Virgin in the Liturgy of the Church,* in MS, 3 (1952), 218–227.
[139] AAS, 46 (1954), 638.
[140] Cf. Pius XII, in AAS, 38 (1946), 266.

In the New Testament we have two texts which are frequently adduced in support of the Catholic thesis. In Luke 1:30-35 the Angel Gabriel announces to Mary that she is to become the Mother of a King who will reign forever. In the twelfth chapter of the Apocalypse Our Lady, symbolizing the Church, is portrayed with the moon under her feet and wearing a crown of twelve stars (v. 1-2), and as the Mother of a Son who will rule all nations; a Son who is taken up to God and to His throne (v. 7).[141]

There are several other Old Testament passages which have been frequently utilized in connection with Mary's Queenship; for example: Psalm 44:10; 3 Kings 2:19; Esther 2:17 and 5:3. However, until it is sufficiently established that the Holy Ghost intended to convey the idea of Mary's Queenship in these passages, we may use them only as adaptations, not as biblical arguments.

V. *The Voice of Tradition.* In the early centuries of the Church we do not find many explicit and clear statements to the effect that Mary is our Queen.[142] But from the 8th century on, the doctrine becomes increasingly evident in the writings of the Fathers. Thus St. Andrew

---

[141] Cf. E. Smith, O.F.M., *The Scriptural Basis for Mary's Queenship,* in MS, 4 (1953), 109–115.

[142] Cf. M. J. Donnelly, S.J., *The Queenship of Mary during the Patristic Period,* in MS, 4 (1953), 82 ff.; H. Barré, C.S.Sp., *La royauté de Marie pendant les neuf premiers siècles,* in RSR, 29 (1939), 129–162; 303–334; A. Luis, C.SS.R., *La realeza de María* (Madrid, 1942), 32–42.

of Crete (d. c. 727), St. Germain of Constantinople (d. 733), St. John Damascene (d. 749) and Eadmer of Canterbury (d. 1124) frequently style Mary "Queen of the universe," "Queen of the human race," etc.[143] In the Middle Ages one of the most articulate champions of Mary's royal dominion was unquestionably St. Bernardine of Siena (d. 1444).[143a] Beginning with the 17th century, we find not only the explicit and frequent statement of the doctrine, but also its theological elaboration. The most important names in this connection are F. Suárez, S.J. (d. 1617), C. de Vega, S.J. (d. 1672), and especially the Augustinian Bartholomew de los Rios (d. 1652).[144] In the 20th century several Marian Congresses and an imposing number of bishops have openly endorsed the thesis while urging the Holy See to honor Mary's Queenship with a liturgical feast similar to that of Christ the King.[145]

VI. *Extent and Nature of Mary's Queenship.* The

[143] St. Andrew, *Orat. 3 in dormit. Deiparae; PG,* 97, 1099; St. Germain, *In praesent. Deiparae; PG,* 98, 303; St. John Damascene, *De fide orthodoxa,* 1, 4, 14; *PG,* 94, 1158–1159; Eadmer of Canterbury, *De excellentia Virginis Mariae,* 11; *PL,* 159, 578.

[143a] *Sermo de gratia et gloria B. Virginis,* cap. 6; *opera omnia,* 2 (Quaracchi, 1950), 377. Cf. likewise Ch. Sericoli, O.F.M., *De regalitate B. M. Virginis juxta auctorum franciscalium doctrinam,* in *Ant,* 30 (1955), 105–118; 221–244.

[144] Suárez, *De mysteriis vitae Christi,* disp. 3, sect. 5, n. 29; *opera omnia,* ed. Vivès, 19 (Paris, 1860), 44; disp. 22, sect. 2, n. 4; *opera omnia,* 19, 327; C. de Vega, *Theologia Mariana,* pal. 27 (Naples, 1866), 2, 346–364; B. de los Rios, *De hierarchia mariana libri sex . . .* (Antwerp, 1641). Cf. W. F. Hill, S.S., *Our Lady's Queenship in the Middle Ages and Modern Times,* in *MS,* 4 (1953), 134–169.

[145] Cf. F. Schmidt, O.F.M.Cap., *Mary's Universal Queenship,* in *Mariology* (Carol), 2, Ch. 13.

commonly received views on the extent and nature of
Mary's Queenship may be summarized as follows:

A. Our Blessed Lady's dominion is as vast as that of
her divine Son. Her Queenship is co-extensive with His
Kingship. Hence, Mary is Queen of *all* rational creatures:
men and angels. She is their Queen "by grace, by divine
relationship, by right of conquest, and by singular election."[146] The title "by right of conquest" may not be so
readily understood by some with regard to the angels.
Nevertheless, if we hold—as many do—that the angels,
too, were redeemed by Christ (in the sense that they
were preserved from falling, in view of His future
merits), then He is their King also by right of conquest,
although in a more sublime way. In this hypothesis,
something similar may be predicated of Our Blessed
Lady, who participated so intimately in her Son's redemptive role with regard to all others.

B. Our Lady's Queenship is primarily of a *spiritual*
nature; its principal sphere of action is the supernatural
order, the order of grace. Secondarily, however, Mary's
Queenship is also *temporal*, even as Christ's Kingship.
Christ, not only as God but also as Man, has a direct,
absolute and unlimited power over all civil rulers, all
civil affairs. He has the absolute right of ownership and
supreme dominion not only over this world of ours and
everything in it, but also over the entire universe. With
and under Christ, Mary is Queen over all these things.

[146] Pius XII, in AAS, 38 (1946), 266.

In a word, she is Queen of *all creation*. However, in order better to fulfill the purpose of the Incarnation, Our Blessed Savior and His Mother—while retaining the *right* to temporal power—voluntarily relinquished the *exercise* of that right.

◄§ Part Two §►

THE SINGULAR PREROGATIVES
OF MARY

We have seen in the first part of this course that Almighty God predestined Our Blessed Lady to a mission which was utterly singular and unique. Since it is fitting that the means be proportionate to the end, it follows logically that Our Lady's personal privileges and prerogatives (the means) must be singular and unique in order to correspond to the end (her mission). The singular prerogatives were conferred on Mary at the beginning, in the course, and at the end of her earthly career. Hence we shall divide this second part of Mariology into three sections, corresponding to these three stages.

SECTION ONE

*Prerogatives Conferred on Mary at the
Beginning of Her Life*

Of the two prerogatives conferred upon
Our Lady at the beginning of her earthly life,
one is negative (immunity from original sin);
the other is positive (fullness of grace). Hence
the two following chapters.

The Immaculate Conception

THE doctrine of Mary's Immaculate Conception was solemnly defined by Pope Pius IX on December 8, 1854 with these words which are taken from the Bull *Ineffabilis Deus* issued by him on that day: "We declare, pronounce and define that the doctrine which holds that the Most Blessed Virgin|Mary, at the first instant of her conception was preserved immune from all stain of sin, by a singular grace and privilege of the Omnipotent God, | in view of the merits of Jesus Christ, the Savior of the human race, was revealed by God and, therefore, must be firmly and constantly believed by all the faithful."[147]

We shall first explain the words of the definition briefly and then proceed to prove the doctrine from Sacred Scripture, Tradition and theological reason.

Article 1

EXPLANATION OF THE DEFINITION

The subject or recipient of this privilege of the Immaculate Conception is the *person* of Mary in the first instant of her *passive* conception. Active conception refers to the generative act by which the parents produce the human foetus; while passive conception refers to the

[147] ADSC, 6, 842; DB, 1641; Palmer, *op. cit.*, 86–87.

time when the human *person* is constituted, namely, when God infuses the human soul into the foetus produced by the parents.[148] All human beings having Adam as their physical and moral head[149] automatically contract original sin in the first instant of their passive conception, which means that they are deprived of the grace which would have been theirs, had Adam remained faithful to God's law. Since Our Blessed Lady, by a unique privilege from God, was not included in the moral headship of Adam, she was never for an instant under the curse of Satan, never for an instant stained with the sin of Adam.

The definition goes on to say that Mary was preserved immune from original sin in view of the merits of Jesus Christ, the Savior of mankind. That means that her preservation was caused by the application to her of the foreseen merits of the Savior. Hence Mary must be said to have been redeemed (or rather: pre-redeemed) by the

[148] Cf. Bonnefoy, *Marie préservée de toute tache du péché originel*, in VII*e* *Congrès Marial National: L'Immaculée Conception* (Lyons, 1955), 187–220, esp. 208–212.

[149] Hence, in our humble opinion, the widespread notion that descent from Adam by way of "ordinary generation," of itself and necessarily, brings about original sin, is theologically inaccurate. The fact that this notion, like many other stereotyped formulas, has been handed down from generation to generation through our manuals, does not make it acceptable. Fortunately, in recent years a growing number of theologians have become aware that the so-called "traditional" views on this point call for a thorough revision. They rightly point out that, of itself, "ordinary" generation is only an occasion with regard to the contraction of original sin; it is the moral headship of Adam which alone *causes* it in us. Thus, in the hypothesis that a child were conceived through a physico-chemical process of generation, he would still have to be baptized to be cleansed from original sin, because of his inclusion in the moral headship of Adam. Cf. Bonnefoy, *Quelques théories modernes du "debitum peccati,"* in *EphM*, 4 (1954), 283.

merits of her Son.[150] The bull also states that this privilege was singular; which means that it cannot be presumed to have been granted to anyone else, either before or after Mary.

According to the definition, the Immaculate Conception is not merely a true doctrine, but a revealed one; in other words, it always formed an integral part of the original deposit of revelation entrusted by God to His Church. However, the bull does not specify how it was revealed by God, namely whether explicitly or implicitly, formally or virtually. The more reasonable interpretation seems to be that it was *formally-implicitly* revealed.[151]

Adversaries of the Doctrine. Before the definition of Pius IX the Immaculate Conception was denied by many and very great Catholic scholars who found it impossible to conciliate this doctrine with the revealed teaching concerning the universality of original sin, and the universality of Christ's Redemption. It was denied also by Luther, Calvin and their followers. After the definition of 1854 it is still rejected by most non-Catholics, Protestants, Rationalists, the sect known as "Old Catholics," and the Greek Orthodox or Schismatics. Their contention is that the doctrine in question does not have the support of either Sacred Scripture or Tradition. We shall attempt to show that it has.

[150] Cf. section on the *debitum peccati*, below.
[151] Cf. A. Wolter, O.F.M., *The Theology of the Immaculate Conception in the Light of "Ineffabilis Deus,"* in MS, 5 (1954), 19–72, esp. 42 ff.

PROOF FROM SACRED SCRIPTURE

While prior to 1854 not a few scholars maintained that Sacred Scripture, taken by itself, did not furnish a cogent argument in favor of the Immaculate Conception, most Catholic theologians now admit that such an argument does exist. In the bull of the definition, Pius IX himself brings forth two biblical passages in particular as containing the doctrine of Mary's original sinlessness, namely: the Protoevangelium (Genesis 3:15), and the Angelic Salutation (Luke 1:28). Let us examine them briefly.

I. *The Protoevangelium.* After the commission of the first sin in the garden of Eden, God addressed Satan (under the appearance of a serpent) with these words: "I will put enmities between thee and the woman, and (between) thy seed and her seed; she (the original Hebrew has "he") shall crush thy head, and thou shalt lie in wait for her (his) heel." We have shown elsewhere[152] that the woman mentioned here is Mary, and that her seed is Christ the Redeemer. Hence we may argue as follows: The enmity established by God between the seed of Satan and Christ is absolute, perpetual and continuous. But the enmity existing between Satan and Mary is *identically the same* enmity as that

---

[152] Cf. above, Part 1, Ch. 2, Art. 1. Cf. also A. Bea, *Bulla "Ineffabilis Deus" et hermeneutica biblica*, in VgI 3 (Rome, 1955), 1–17; B. Mariani, O.F.M., *L'Immacolata nel Protoevangelo: Gen. 3:15*, ibid. 29–99.

existing between Christ and the seed of Satan;[153] therefore, it follows that the former is just as absolute, perpetual and continuous as the latter. Now, if Mary had
been, even for a single instant, under the dominion of
Satan (through sin), her enmity with him would not
have been perpetual and absolute. Therefore, she was
always an enemy of the devil, always a friend of God.

It should be noted that the above argument is based
on the first part of the Protoevangelium. The second
part (i.e., "*she* shall crush thy head") does not furnish
a direct biblical argument in favor of the Immaculate
Conception because, according to the original Hebrew
text, the triumph or victory over Satan, as expressed by
the crushing of his head, is directly attributed to the
seed of the woman (i.e., Christ), not to the woman herself. However, Pius IX in his *Ineffabilis Deus*, and more
recently Pius XII in his *Munificentissimus Deus* have
interpreted the Protoevangelium as implying Mary's
intimate share in Christ's total victory over Satan. Now,
since Christ's victory over Satan coincides with His
redemptive work, and since the Redemption means the
utter destruction of sin, it follows that Mary, too, as
Coredemptrix, helped destroy the power of sin, and
therefore, could not have been herself tainted by sin.

II. *The Angelic Salutation.* On the day of the
Annunciation the Angel Gabriel addressed these words
to Mary: "Hail, full of grace, the Lord is with thee"

[153] Pius XII, *Munificentissimus Deus*, in AAS, 42 (1950), 769.

(Luke 1:28). It must be borne in mind that these words, taken in themselves, do not necessarily prove that Mary was conceived without sin. They would still be true if Our Lady had been "full of grace" only from the time of the Annunciation, and not from the very beginning of her existence. However, understood in the light of Catholic tradition, the words spoken by the angel do refer to a fullness without time-limit, a fullness of grace which extends to the very first moment of Mary's existence. The argument, therefore, is not purely and exclusively biblical, but biblico-traditional.

It must be noted also that the original Greek text, as written by St. Luke, does not use the adjective "full," but rather the perfect participle of the verb "to endow with grace." Hence, a more accurate translation of the Greek expression (*kekaritomene*) would be: ". . . thou who hast been graced." This rendering does not in the least diminish the force of the argument; on the contrary, it seems to strengthen it, because, according to the Greek construction, the angel would be saying to Mary the equivalent of this: "Hail, thou, the graced one, *par excellence.*" At any rate, it is interesting to note that the special commission of theologians charged by Pius IX with the task of drafting the bull of the definition admitted that the dogma of the Immaculate Conception did not rest on this text alone, but principally on the Protoevangelium.[154]

[154] Cf. V. Sardi, *La solenne definizione del dogma dell'Immacolato Concepimento di Maria Santissima. Atti e documenti . . .* , 1 (Rome, 1905), 796–800.

Article 3

THE ARGUMENT FROM TRADITION

The witnesses of Tradition relative to the Immaculate Conception may be conveniently divided into the following four periods:

I. the period of implicit belief (1st to 4th century);

II. the period of gradual development (4th to 11th century);

III. the period of controversy (11th to 15th century);

IV. the period of universal belief (15th to 19th century).

I. *From the Beginning to the Fourth Century.* The Fathers and ecclesiastical writers of the first three centuries may be said to have accepted the doctrine of the Immaculate Conception implicitly. By this is meant simply that the doctrine was *implied* in their teaching concerning (*a*) Mary's role as the New Eve, and (*b*) the unparalleled holiness of the Mother of God.

A. The striking contrast between Eve and Mary is frequently emphasized in the writings of the Fathers and other early Christian authors. They taught that, as Eve together with Adam had been the source and the cause of sin for their posterity, so Mary together with Christ was the wellspring and cause of grace and holiness for the human race. Sometimes the comparison is drawn, not by way of antithesis, but by way of similarity. In this sense they compare Mary with Eve before the latter's fall, that is, while Eve was still in the state of original justice and grace.[155]

B. Mary's unparalleled sanctity was often described by early writers in a variety of forceful expressions which seem to imply her immunity from original sin. Thus, she is styled "all-holy," "all-pure," "most innocent," "a miracle of grace," "purer than the angels," "altogether without stain," etc. They failed to specify, however, that she had enjoyed these attributes from the beginning of her existence.[156]

II. *From the Fourth to the Eleventh Century.* During this period the belief in Mary's original purity begins to receive a clearer formulation. We shall give but a summary of this gradual development, century by century.

A. *Fourth Century.* In the East we have the significant words of St. Ephraem the Syrian (d. 373): "Those two innocent . . . women, Mary and Eve, had been made (created) utterly equal, but afterwards one became the cause of our death, the other the cause of our life."[157] And again in one of St. Ephraem's hymns Our Lord is addressed with these words: "Thou and Thy Mother are the only ones who are immune from all stain; for there is no spot in Thee, O Lord, nor any taint

[155] Cf. footnote 111, above; also Burghardt, *Mary in Eastern Patristic Thought*, in *Mariology* (Carol), 2, Ch. 3.

[156] Cf. G. E. Price, *The Term "Immaculate" in Early Greek Writers*, in *AER*, 31 (December, 1904), 545–556. Cf. G. Söll, S.D.B., *Elementa evolutionis in historia dogmatis Immaculatae Conceptionis B. M. Virginis ante Concilium Ephesinum*, in *VgI* 4 (Rome, 1955), 1–9.

[157] St. Ephraem, *Sermones exegetici; opera omnia syriace et latine*, 2 (Rome, 1740), 327.

in Thy Mother."[158] In the West we have the testimony of St. Ambrose of Milan (d. 379), who refers to Mary as "free from all stain of sin."[159]

B. *Fifth Century.* Among the Eastern Fathers we may mention Theodotus, bishop of Ancyra (d. *c.* 445), according to whom Our Lady is "an innocent virgin, spotless, holy in soul and body, like a lily budding in the midst of thorns, who did not know the evils of Eve; . . . who was a daughter of Adam, but unlike him."[160]

In the West we encounter at this time the much controverted testimony of St. Augustine, bishop of Hippo (d. 430). In one place, while admitting that all the just of the Old Testament had sinned during their lives, he adds: . . . "except the holy Virgin Mary, concerning whom, out of respect for the Lord, I wish to raise no question when speaking of sin."[161] From the context, however, it is evident that the holy Doctor is speaking, not of original sin, but of actual, personal sins. In another place, answering Julian of Eclanum, who had accused him of making Mary a subject of the devil, St. Augustine replies: "We do not subject Mary to the devil owing to the law of birth; but [the reason we do not, is]

[158] *Carmina nisibena,* 27; ed. G. Bickel (Leipzig, 1866), 40. Cf. I. Ortiz de Urbina, *¿Vale el testimonio de San Efrén en favor de la Inmaculada?,* in *EE,* 28 (1954), 417–422.

[159] St. Ambrose, *Expositio in ps. 118, serm.* 22, n. 30; *PL,* 15, 1599. Cf. however, *Expositio in ps. 48,* n. 13, *PL,* 14, 1216, where St. Ambrose states that *all,* with the *sole* exception of Christ, were subject to Adam's sin.

[160] Theodotus, *Hom. 6, in S. Deiparam; PG,* 77, 1428.

[161] St. Augustine, *De natura et gratia,* cap. 36, n. 42; *PL,* 44, 267.

because this law (of birth) is destroyed by the grace of being born again."[162] The text is not particularly clear. Much has been written about it, and various interpretations have been offered.[163] Some say that Augustine is speaking here of Mary's birth, not of her conception. Others answer that, from the context, the word "birth," as used here, has the meaning of "coming into being." Besides, they argue, if the "grace of rebirth" mentioned in the text had been a grace freeing Mary from original sin and not preserving her from it, then Mary would have been a subject of the devil for some time, which is precisely what St. Augustine meant to reject.[164]

C. *Sixth Century.* Worthy of mention is the following testimony of Severus, bishop of Antioch (d. 538): "She (Mary) . . . formed part of the human race, and was of the same essence as we, although she was pure from all taint and immaculate."[165]

D. *Seventh Century.* St. Sophronius, patriarch of Jerusalem (d. 638), seems to be the first to speak of a preventive purification, when he addresses Mary with these words: "Thou hast found the grace which no one has received . . . No one has been pre-purified besides thee."[166]

[162] *Opus imperf. contra Julianum*, lib. 4, cap. 122; PL, 45, 1418.
[163] Cf. Burghardt, *Mary in Western Patristic Thought*, 144–145, and the literature indicated therein.
[164] Cf. Ch. Boyer, S.J., *Bulletin augustinien*, in Gr, 14 (1933), 93–96; id., *La controverse sur l'opinion de saint Augustin touchant la Conception de la Vierge*, in VgI 4 (Rome, 1955), 48–60; and I. M. Dietz, *Ist die Hl. Jungfrau nach Augustinus "immaculata ab initio"?*, ibid. 61–112.
[165] St. Severus, *Hom. cathedralis* 67; PO, 8, 350.
[166] St. Sophronius, *Orat. in Deiparae Annunt.*, 25; PG, 87, 3246–3247.

E. *Eighth Century*. St. Andrew, archbishop of Crete (d. 740), tells us that "the Redeemer of the human race, wishing to introduce a new birth and reformation in place of the first, chooses in all nature this pure and entirely Immaculate Virgin in order to bring about His own Incarnation, just as He had formerly fashioned the first Adam from a virgin and unspotted clay."[167] Elsewhere, recalling that every human being must pass through death, the Saint states: "It is evident that she too (Mary) must have been subject to the same law (of death) as we are . . . , although in a more excellent manner and for a higher reason, quite different from the reason that leads us to that fatal end."[168] Mary died, then, not because of original sin, but, as the Saint says a few lines before, "in order to pay tribute to the laws of nature."

F. *Ninth Century*. In the East, St. Tarasius, patriarch of Constantinople (d. 806) assures us that Our Lady was "predestined from the creation of the world and chosen from among all generations to be the immaculate dwelling place of the Word. . . . Is she not the immaculate oblation of human nature?"[169] More important still is the testimony of the monk Theognostes of Constantinople (died toward the end of the ninth century), because he is the *first* writer who clearly mentions Mary's immaculate origin. He writes: "It was indeed fitting that she who *from the beginning had been conceived by a*

[167] St. Andrew, Hom. 1 in nativ. Deiparae; PG, 97, 813–814.
[168] Hom. 1 in dormit.; PG, 97, 1053.
[169] St. Tarasius, Hom. in praesent. Deiparae, 13; PG, 98, 1497.

sanctifying action . . . should also have a holy death.
. . . Holy the beginning . . . , holy the end, holy her whole
existence."[170] In the West we have another significant
statement from the pen of St. Paschasius Radbertus
(d. 860). According to him, Mary was "incorrupt, incon-
taminated and untouched by the *original* contagion."[171]

G. *Tenth Century.* Worthy of mention during this
time are the two following passages. Peter, bishop of
Argos (d. after 920): "Let us all rejoice seeing that in
the womb of Ann is planted the first offspring of the
original nobility of our nature."[172] And John Geometra
(d. after 989): "A divine virtue has veritably presided
over the formation and perfect embellishment of this
(Mary's) nature *from the beginning.*"[173]

III. *From the Eleventh to the Fifteenth Century.*
This is generally referred to as the "controversy period."
However, we must bear in mind that the debate took
place in the West; the Eastern writers of this time proclaimed the Immaculate Conception louder than ever
before. Hence, a distinction is imperative.

A. *In the East,* Theophilactus, archbishop of Ochrida
(died toward the end of the 11th century), has this to
say: "It was necessary that she who, on account of her
purity and sanctity, ranked above all nature, and who has
been justified (sanctified) in the womb of her mother,

[170] Theognostes, *Hom. in dormit. Deiparae; PO,* 16, 457.
[171] St. Paschasius, *De partu Virginis,* 1; *PL,* 120, 1375.
[172] Peter of Argos, *In concept. B. Annae,* 2; *PG,* 104, 1353.
[173] John Geometra, *Hom. in dormit. Deiparae;* codex Vaticanus, 504,
fol. 175v–176r; ref. from M. Jugie, *L'Immaculée Conception dans
l'Ecriture Sainte et dans la tradition orientale* (Rome, 1952), 186.

should escape the rigor of a law which was not made for the just but only for sinners."[174] During this same period the Immaculate Conception was quite clearly alluded to by John Phournes (died at the beginning of the 12th century), Neophitus Reclusus (d. c. 1220), Germain II, patriarch of Constantinople (d. 1240), and particularly Nicholas Cabasilas (d. after 1396), and George Scholarios (d. after 1472). The last two mentioned taught the doctrine as explicitly as we do today.[175]

B. *In the West*, however, we note the beginning of a long and bitter controversy which was to engage the most brilliant scholars of the period. The dispute actually arose in England at the beginning of the 12th century when some objected to the celebration of a feast in honor of the Conception. The feast was immediately defended by Eadmer of Canterbury (d. 1124) and Osbert of Clare (d. c. 1137), who are also important witnesses in favor of the doctrine of Mary's original sinlessness.[176] In the year 1140 St. Bernard of Clairvaux (d. 1153) wrote his now famous letter to the canons of Lyons, who had begun to celebrate the same feast. In this letter St. Bernard vehemently protests against the

[174] Theophilactus, *Hom. in praesent. Deiparae; PG,* 126, 137.

[175] These and several other testimonies may be read in Jugie, *op. cit.,* 200–204, 209–216, 246–262, 301–307.

[176] Eadmer, *Tractatus de conceptione S. Mariae,* ed. Thurston-Slater, (Freiburg, 1904), 9; Osbert of Clare, *Epist. ad Anselmum abbatem S. Edmundi;* in Thurston's ed. of Eadmer's *Tractatus,* appendix A, 53–59. Cf. G. Geenen, O.P., *Eadmer, le premier théologien de l'Immaculée Conception,* in VgI 5 (1955), 90–136; G. Gagov, O.F.M.Conv., *L'ambiente liturgico e culturale inglese a favore dell'Immacolata e Giovanni Duns Scoto, O. Min.,* ibid., 74–89; H. F. Davis, *Theologia Immaculatae Conceptionis apud primos defensores, scl. in Anglia, saec. XII,* ibid. 1–12.

absurdity of celebrating a feast in honor of something which was not holy but connected with sin (concupiscence), such as the act by which Mary's parents had conceived her. He argued further: "If Mary could not be sanctified before her conception, since she did not as yet exist, nor in the act of conception itself, on account of the sin (concupiscence) involved therein, it follows that she was sanctified in the womb *after* conception; and this, since she was cleansed from sin, rendered her birth holy, not her conception."[177]

This letter, owing to the authority enjoyed by St. Bernard, exerted great influence upon the theologians of subsequent centuries, the majority of whom (at least up to the 15th century) openly denied Mary's prerogative. Among these we may mention such great masters as Alexander of Hales (d. 1245), St. Bonaventure (d. 1274), St. Albert the Great (d. 1280), St. Thomas Aquinas (d. 1274), Henry of Ghent (d. 1293), and Peter of Tarantasia (d. 1276), who later became Pope Innocent V.[178]

[177] St. Bernard, *Epist. 174, ad canonicos lugdunenses; PL,* 182, 332–336. Cf. L. Modrić, O.F.M., *Doctrina de Conceptione B. V. Mariae in controversia saec. XII,* in VgI 5 (Rome, 1955), 13–73.
[178] Alexander of Hales, *Summa Theologica,* lib. 3, *de Verbo Incarnato,* tract. 2, q. 2, membr. 2, cap. 1, art. 4; (ed. Quaracchi, 1948), 4, 118; St. Bonaventure, *In 3 Sent.,* dist. 3, pars 1, art. 1, q. 2 (Quaracchi, 1887), 3, 67–69; Albert the Great, *In 3 Sent.,* dist. 3, art. 5; St. Thomas, *In 3 Sent.,* dist. 3, p. 1, art. 2; id., *Summa Theologica,* III, 27, 2, ad 2; Henry of Ghent, *Quodlibet* 15, fol. 584v (Paris, 1518), 13; Peter of Tarantasia, *In 3 Sent.,* dist. 3, p. 1 (Toulouse, 1652), 3, 18. On the controversy over the genuine teaching of St. Thomas, cf. Roschini, *La Mariologia di San Tommaso* (Rome, 1950), 195–237; and also H. Storff, O.F.M., *The Immaculate Conception. The Teaching of St. Thomas, St. Bonaventure, and Bl. J. Duns Scotus* . . . (San Francisco, 1925). The

The main reasons hindering the Scholastics from accepting the Immaculate Conception were these: 1) the Augustinian theory[179] according to which original sin had infected the human flesh which, in turn, automatically infected the soul at the time of its infusion in the body; and 2) the biblical passages, especially Romans 5, relative to the universality of original sin, and the universality of Christ's Redemption.

However, not all the theologians of this period shared the views of the masters. Among the more notable exceptions we may mention St. Peter Paschasius, O. de M. (d. 1300), William of Ware, O.F.M. (d. 1300), and Raymond Lull, T.O.R. (d. 1315).[180]

But the one who has been traditionally regarded (indirectly, even by his archenemies) as the most illustrious champion of the Immaculate Conception is the Franciscan theologian, Ven. John Duns Scotus (d. 1308), rightly styled the *Marian Doctor*. Actually, his merit lies

---

book is a devastating reply to P. Lumbreras, O.P., *St. Thomas and the Immaculate Conception*, in HPR, 24 (December, 1923), 253–263.

[179] Cf. St. Augustine, *Contra Julianum*, cap. 15, n. 54; PL, 44, 814.

[180] St. Peter Paschasius, *Disputatio cum hebraeis* (written around 1299), according to V. Mancini, *Il primo difensore dell'Immacolata Concezione è stato un Mercedario: S. Pietro Pascasio* (Naples, 1939); cf. Roschini, *Mariologia*, 2, part 2, 63–64; William of Ware, *Quaestiones disputatae de Immaculata Conceptione B.M. Virginis* (Quaracchi, 1904), 1–11; Raymond Lull, *Disputatio Eremitae et Raymundi super aliquibus dubiis quaestionibus Sententiarum Magistri Petri Lombardi* (written in Paris, 1298), p. 96; cf. X. M. Le Bachelet, S.J., art. *Immaculée Conception*, in DTC, 7, 1062–1063. For a lengthy treatment of this whole period, cf. Francisco de Guimaraens, O.F.M.Cap., *La doctrine des théologiens sur l'Immaculée Conception de 1250 à 1350*, in EF (December, 1952), 181–203; (June, 1953), 23–51; (December, 1955), 167–187. Cf. also L. Modrić, O.F.M., *De Petro Compostellano qui primus assertor Immaculatae Conceptionis dicitur*, in Ant, 29 (1954), 563–572.

primarily in this that he successfully refuted the chief objections which had been raised against the doctrine, thus proving that Mary's privilege was possible. To the reasons mentioned above against Mary's immunity from sin, Scotus answered substantially as follows:

(1) Original sin does not come about through the transmission of guilt from the infected body to the soul upon the latter's creation and infusion.[181] Original sin consists rather in the privation of sanctifying grace which, owing to Adam's sin, is lacking in the soul at the time of its creation.

(2) He who descends from Adam by way of ordinary generation does contract original sin, *unless* he be preserved by grace from contracting it, as in the case of Our Blessed Lady.[182]

(3) The fact that Mary did not contract original sin does not mean that she is not indebted to Christ's Redemption. On the contrary, she owes more to that Redemption than anyone else. In the case of all others, Christ's redemptive grace destroys sin *after* it has done its harm, while in Mary's case the grace of Christ *prevents* sin from ever reaching her soul.[183]

The question may perhaps be asked: But is it not arbitrary to presuppose this different mode of Redemption for Mary and the rest of mankind? In other words, on what grounds can we postulate this twofold manner

---

[181] Scotus, *Opus Oxoniense*, lib. 3, dist. 3, p. 1; ed. C. Balić, O.F.M., J. D. *Scoti Theologiae marianae elementa* (Sibenici, 1933), 27.

[182] Scotus, *ibid.*; ed. Balić, 34–35.

[183] Scotus, *ibid.*; ed. Balić, 35–36.

of redemption? For Scotus, this recourse to a *pre-redemption* in Mary's favor is not arbitrary, but seems to be demanded by the very perfection of Christ's redemptive grace. His argument is briefly formulated as follows: "He who is the most perfect Mediator (Redeemer) has the most perfect possible act of mediating (redeeming) in regard to some person on whose behalf he mediates. Therefore, Christ had the most perfect act of mediating possible with regard to some person whose Mediator He was. But He had no more exalted degree (of mediating) regarding any other person than Mary; therefore, etc. But this would not be, had He not merited her preservation from original sin."[184]

From motives of humility, and out of reverence toward the great many scholars who held the opposite view, Scotus worded his defense of Mary's privilege in extremely moderate language. For this reason, after giving the various solutions, pro and con, in this connection, he simply states: "If it does not go counter to the authority of the Church or the authority of Scripture, it seems *probable* that we should attribute to Mary that which is more excellent."[185]

[184] Scotus, *ibid.*; ed. Balić, 22–23. On the force of this argument, questioned by a few, cf. C. Koser, O.F.M., *A teologia da Imaculada em Duns Scotus*, in *REB*, 14 (1954), 610–676, esp. 638.

[185] Scotus, *ibid.*; ed. Balić, 31. It is obvious that in this statement, for all the cautiousness in the wording, Scotus declares himself favorable to the Immaculate Conception. Concerning similarly timid expressions of Scotus, and their plausible explanation from other manuscripts, cf. Koser, *art. cit.*, 642–648. For an unfavorable explanation, cf. Roschini, *Duns Scoto e l'Immacolata*, in *Mm*, 17 (1955), 183–252, esp. 195–203. From the "*videtur probabile*" ("it *seems* probable") of Scotus, Roschini concludes that the Subtle Doctor was not sure which side of the con-

We must bear in mind that the primary task of a theologian at that time was to prove, not so much that the Immaculate Conception was a fact or a revealed truth, but rather that it was possible. It was the very possibility of the fact that was emphatically denied by his mighty adversaries, and Scotus naturally directed his efforts to that particular phase of the problem. Hence it was he who, by demolishing the objections of the opponents, helped clear the way for the further studies which eventually culminated in the papal definition of 1854.[186]

After Scotus' death, during the remainder of the 14th century, the question of the Immaculate Conception continued to divide Catholic theologians into two groups: in favor of it were a growing number of Franciscans, a few Augustinians, Dominicans, Carmelites, Servites and secular priests;[187] against it, the majority of

---

troversy he favored. May we note that elsewhere (lib. 3, dist. 8; ed. Balić, 43) Scotus states without any *videtur* or hesitation: "Est etiam [in coelo] beatifica Mater Dei, quae numquam fuit inimica actualiter ratione peccati actualis, nec originaliter ratione peccati originalis, fuisset tamen nisi fuisset praeservata." A scholarly and exhaustive answer to Roschini's article has just been published by Father Balić under the title *Joannes Duns Scotus et historia Immaculatae Conceptionis*, in Ant 30 (1955), 349–488. Incidentally, the author also shows that, in view of recent scientific investigations, the article by Francisco de Guimaraens, already alluded to, can no longer be considered reliable in every respect.

[186] Cf. Balić, *Il reale contributo di G. Scoto nella questione dell' Immacolata Concezione*, in Ant, 29 (1954), 475–496.

[187] Cf. Francisco de Guimaraens, *art. cit.*, and Roschini, *art. cit.*, 217–218, where a summary is given. According to Roschini (*ibid.*, 218), no Servite was ever against the doctrine. The author does not mention how many of his confreres wrote theological commentaries, either before or after Scotus.

theologians, including the men who later became Popes John XXII, Benedict XII, and Clement VI.[188] The open controversies between these two groups often reached such a degree of violence that the civil and ecclesiastical authorities had to intervene, as in the notorious case of John of Montesono [Monzón], O.P., condemned by Pope Clement VII in the year 1389.[189]

IV. *From the Fifteenth to the Nineteenth Century.* In spite of heavy opposition, the doctrine of Mary's original purity gradually succeeded in winning so many adherents, that by the beginning of the 15th century it was already considered by some "the common opinion" among theologians. An exception must be made for the Dominicans, who continued their attacks by appealing to the authority of St. Thomas. In order better to follow the swift progress made by the doctrine during this period, these six stages of evolution will be outlined: a) the Council of Basle; b) the intervention of Sixtus IV; c) the Council of Trent; d) the decrees of St. Pius V; e) the intervention of 17th century popes; and f) Rome's final decision.

A. *The Council of Basle.* In the year 1439 the Council of Basle, after endless discussions between Dominicans and Franciscans,[190] finally issued a decree declaring that

---

[188] Cf. Le Bachelet, *art. cit.*, 1079–1081.

[189] Cf. Roschini, *Mariologia*, 2, part 2, 70.

[190] Cf. H. Ameri, O.F.M., *Doctrina theologorum de Immaculata B. V. Mariae Conceptione tempore Concilii Basileensis* (Rome, 1954), 7–26.

the doctrine of the Immaculate Conception was con-
sonant with Catholic faith, right reason and Sacred
Scripture; that it was to be held by all as the official
teaching of the Church, and that no one should be
allowed to teach or preach anything to the contrary.[191]
It so happens that, at that time, the council had been
placed under an anathema by Pope Eugene IV, and
hence the above conciliar declaration had no juridical
binding force. Nevertheless, the decree revealed the mind
of the majority of those present and, as such, gave considerable impetus to the movement in favor of Mary's
privilege. Notwithstanding this significant step forward,
the opposition increased in vehemence. Among the adversaries, perhaps the most notorious was the Dominican
Vincent Bandelli (later general of his Order) who in
1475 wrote a virulent book attempting to prove that the
doctrine of the Immaculate Conception was impious,
heretical, contrary to sound reason and the teaching of
the Church.[192] It was at this time that the popes began
to intervene directly in favor of Mary's prerogative.[193]

B. *Intervention of Sixtus IV*. The first pope to take a
definite stand on the matter was Sixtus IV, O.F.M. Conv.
In his apostolic constitution *Cum praecelsa*, issued on
February 27, 1477, he officially and solemnly approved
the office of the Conception, granting indulgences to

[191] Mansi, 29, 182 f.
[192] Bandelli, *Libellus recolectorius auctoritatum de veritate conceptionis B. V. Mariae* (Milan, 1475).
[193] Cf. A. Robichaud, S.M., *The Immaculate Conception in the
Magisterium of the Church Before 1854*, in MS, 5 (1954), 73–145,
esp. 95 ff.

those who recited it or attended the Mass in honor of the mystery.[194] Bandelli, however, reiterated his previous attacks in a new book (1481) in which he endeavored to distort the obvious meaning of the Pope's document. Sixtus IV soon retorted with the bull *Grave nimis* (1482) in which he threatened to excommunicate the dissenters and those who charged their opponents with heresy.[195] This second papal intervention did much to quiet the contention, although it did not succeed in persuading Bandelli and his followers to discontinue their persistent opposition.

C. *The Council of Trent.* A fresh and vigorous impetus was given the cause of Our Lady when in the year 1546 many of the bishops and theologians attending the Council of Trent expressed the desire to see the Immaculate Conception defined as a dogma of faith. The Council, however, in order to preserve peace among Catholics, did not take that final step, but simply issued the significant declarations: "It is not the intention of this Holy Synod to include the Blessed and Immaculate Virgin Mary, Mother of God, in the decree which deals with original sin. . . ."[196]

D. *Decree of St. Pius V.* In 1567 the Dominican Pope, St. Pius V, condemned one of the propositions of Baius

[194] Mansi, 32 (Paris-Leipzig, 1901), 373–374. On Sixtus IV, cf. Ch. Sericoli, O.F.M., *Immaculata B. M. Virginis Conceptio juxta Xysti IV constitutiones* (Rome, 1945).

[195] Mansi, 32, 374–375.

[196] Conc. Trid., sess. 5; DB, 792. Cf. M. Tognetti, O.S.M., *L'Immacolata al Concilio Tridentino*, in *Mm*, 15 (1953), 304–374; 555–586; J. Sagüés, S.J., *Trento y la Inmaculada. Naturaleza del dogma mariano*, in *EE*, 28 (1954), 323–367.

which read: "No one but Christ was without original sin, and therefore the Blessed Virgin died in consequence of the sin contracted through Adam, and endured afflictions of this life, like the rest of the just, in punishment for actual and original sin."[197]

E. *Intervention of Seventeenth Century Popes.* In the course of the 17th century we have not less than four important pronouncements from the Supreme Pontiffs on behalf of the Immaculate Conception. In 1616 Paul V issued strict orders forbidding anyone to deny Mary's privilege in public.[198] A few years later, in 1622, Pope Gregory XV went a step further and forbade the denial of the doctrine even in private. As a special favor, the Pope exempted the Dominicans from observing this decree.[199] In 1661 Pope Alexander VII, in his apostolic constitution *Sollicitudo omnium ecclesiarum,* further determined the object of the feast of the Immaculate Conception and renewed the severe sanctions of his predecessors against the adversaries of the doctrine.[200] In 1708 Pope Clement XI, by his constitution *Commissi Nobis,* made the feast a holy day of obligation.[201]

After all these papal pronouncements, not only did the

[197] DB, 1073.
[198] Cf. *Bullarium Privilegiorum ac Diplomatum Romanorum Pontificum,* 5, part 4, 234–235; ref. from Robichaud, *art. cit.,* 113.
[199] *Bullarium* . . . , 45–46. On the decrees of the Holy Office, issued under Pope Urban VIII (1623–1644), cf. I. Iparraguirre, S.J., *Pareceres encontrados sobre la definibilidad de la Inmaculada en el siglo XVII,* in *EE,* 28 (1954), 612–623.
[200] *Bullarium* . . . , 6, part 5, 182–184; Robichaud, *art. cit.,* 118–122.
[201] *Bullarium* . . . , 11, part 1, 206; Robichaud, *art. cit.,* 125.

opposition gradually lose much of its verve (even among the Dominicans), but an ever increasing number of bishops, kings, religious orders and universities began to address petitions to Rome urging that the doctrine of the Immaculate Conception be solemnly declared a dogma of faith. As customary, Rome proceeded very cautiously and very slowly, with the result that the final decision did not come forth until nearly two hundred years later.

F. *Rome's Final Decision.* This unique privilege was reserved for the saintly Pius IX. In 1849, as a preliminary step, he addressed a letter to all the bishops of the world asking for their opinion regarding the definability of the Immaculate Conception.[202] Of the 665 bishops who answered, 570 were favorable, seven or eight were opposed, and the rest were doubtful as to the opportuneness of the proposed definition.[203] Finally, on December 8, 1854, amid the universal jubilation of all true Catholics, Pius IX solemnly defined the doctrine as an article of our faith.

SCHOLION. *The Feast of the Conception.*

In the Eastern Church a distinct liturgical feast began to be celebrated in the second half of the 7th century

[202] Enc. *Ubi primum,* February 2, 1849; text in Sardi, *op. cit.* 1, 571–574.

[203] These episcopal letters, and many other relative testimonies are published in the collection *Pareri dell'Episcopato Cattolico . . . sulla definizione dogmatica dell'Immacolato Concepimento della Beata Vergine Maria,* 10 vols. (Rome, 1851–1854).

under the name "Conception of Saint Ann." Within a couple of centuries, this feast was universally kept throughout the East.[204]

In the Western Church the same feast began to be celebrated around the 8th century in England, and in the 9th century in Sicily and Naples.[205]

What was the precise object of this original feast? It did not correspond exactly and in every point (as some have thought) to the feast now celebrated on December 8; nor, again, was it totally different, as others have claimed. Judging from the sermons preached on that day and the liturgical books used for the occasion, we gather that the feast had for its object the announcement made by the angel to Joachim and Ann concerning Our Lady's conception. In other words, there was a threefold element in the complex object of the feast: (1) the angel's announcement of the conception; (2) the miracle of an active conception in the sterile womb of St. Ann; and (3) the coming into existence (passive conception) of the future Mother of God.[206]

[204] Cf. Jugie, op. cit., 135–45.
[205] Cf. S. Daly, O.S.B., Mary in the Western Liturgy, in Mariology (Carol), 1, 254–260; M. Cecchin, O.S.M., L'Immacolata nella liturgia occidentale anteriore al secolo XIII (Rome, 1943); H. Thurston, S.J., The Irish Origins of Our Lady's Conception Feast, in Mth, 103 (1904), 449–465. For the feast in Spain, cf. L. Frias, S.J., Antiguedad de la fiesta de la Inmaculada Concepción en las iglesias de España, in MC, 22 (1954), 31–85.
[206] Cf. Jugie, op. cit., 137–138.

Article 4

PROOF OF THE DOGMA FROM THEOLOGICAL REASON

Human reason alone cannot prove apodictically that Our Lady was conceived without original sin. At most it can advance arguments of fittingness (of varying degrees) in favor of the doctrine. Nevertheless, by means of the analogy of faith, that is, by comparing Catholic doctrines among themselves and examining their mutual relationship, the human intellect may arrive at a new truth by way of an analysis or at least a logical deduction. In the specific case of the Immaculate Conception some authors are of the opinion that this doctrine may be arrived at through such a logical process. Others, on the contrary, believe that even the most cogent argument from theological reason does not exceed the limits of high fittingness in this connection. Be that as it may, we shall now proceed to summarize these arguments reducing them to the following three:

I. *Mary's Singular Predestination.* Some theologians reason thus: Our Lady's predestination to the divine Maternity *preceded* the predestination of Adam (with a logical priority, not a priority of time). Hence, God foresaw Our Lady and her dignity *before* He foresaw that Adam would sin and involve his posterity in that sin. This being so, Adam's disobedience could in no way affect the status of Our Lady. To assume that it did, would be to attribute a change of mind to the immutable God, for in this hypothesis God would have first foreseen Mary's conception endowed with grace, and subsequently He would have foreseen that same conception deprived of grace.

II. *Mary's Divine Motherhood.* Our Blessed Lady was chosen by God from all eternity to be the worthy Mother of His Son. Now if Mary had been in sin, even for an instant, she would have been (at least during that instant) an enemy of God, which would certainly render her unworthy to be the Mother of God. Besides, since the shame of a parent brings disgrace upon the child, original sin in Mary would have detracted from the honor due to Christ. Again, as Mother of God, Mary's exalted dignity by far outranks the dignity of all creatures; but Eve and the angels began their existence in the state of holiness; therefore, with much more reason should Mary be accorded a similar privilege.

III. *Mary's Coredemption.* As shown elsewhere, Our Blessed Lady was charged by God with the office of Coredemptrix of mankind with and under Christ. As Coredemptrix, it was Mary's sublime task to offer satisfaction for Adam's sin and thus reconcile the human race with God. Hence we cannot suppose that Mary herself was, even for a moment, in need of satisfaction or reconciliation owing to the stain of original sin in her soul. According to Cardinal Lépicier and others, this is the most cogent theological argument in favor of the Immaculate Conception.[207]

APPENDIX I

The Alleged Debt of Sin in Our Blessed Lady

By "debt" of original sin is meant the universal need or necessity of being subjected to it. According to the explanation generally given, this "debt" or necessity arises from two facts: (*a*) being a member of the human race according to the ordinary laws of propagation; and (*b*) being included in the wilful act of disobedience by which Adam lost the grace of God for the whole human race. The former fact induces a *remote* necessity (*debitum remotum*) to incur original sin; the latter fact creates a proximate necessity (*debitum proximum*) to contract it.[208] When applying this distinction to Our Lady, theologians are divided into the three following groups:

[207] A. H. M. Lépicier, O.S.M., *Tractatus de Beatissima Virgine Maria Matre Dei*, 5th ed. (Rome, 1926), 172; id., *L'Immacolata Corredentrice, Mediatrice* (Rome, 1928), 86–90.

[208] For a brief, but very clear explanation of the *debitum*, cf. J. A. de Aldama, S.J., *Mariologia*, in *Sacrae Theologiae Summa*, written by the Spanish Jesuits, 3 (Madrid, 1950), 311–314. For reasons to be explained subsequently, we believe that there is only one kind of debt, namely, the one called "proximate." The so-called "remote" debt does not actually give rise to any necessity to contract original sin. On the amazing multiplicity of distinctions introduced by theologians in this connection, cf. Balić, *De debito peccati originalis in B. Virgine Maria* . . . (Rome, 1941), 11–24. For a more detailed history of this thorny question, cf. Bonnefoy, *La negación del "debitum peccati" en María. Panorama histórico*, in VyV, 12 (1954), 103–171; J. M. Delgado Varela, O. de M., *Exención del débito según los mariólogos españoles de 1600 a 1650*, in *EphM*, 1 (1951), 501–526.

A. Those who claim that, being a member of the human race by way of ordinary generation, and being included in the will of Adam as representative of the race, Our Lady *should have* contracted original sin, if God had not miraculously suspended the application of the general law in her case. Hence, according to them, Mary contracted the *proximate* debt of sin. This is the opinion of Suárez, Pesch, Aldama and others.[209]

B. Those who hold that, being a member of the human race by way of ordinary generation, Mary should have been included in the representative will of Adam, but God exempted her from this, and hence from actually contracting original sin. In this view, therefore, Mary should have contracted a proximate debt of sin, but actually contracted only a *remote* debt. Such is the opinion of Mazzella, Janssens, Roschini, and many others.[210]

C. Those who believe that God exempted Our Blessed Lady from every necessity of contracting original sin, whatever the source whence that necessity might arise. In other words, Mary had neither the remote nor the proximate debt of sin. This opinion, cherished prin-

[209] Suárez, *De vitiis et peccatis*, disp. 9, sect. 4, n. 10; ed. Vivès, 4, 614; Ch. Pesch, S.J., *Compendium theologiae dogmaticae*, 6th ed., 3 (Freiburg, 1940), 95; Aldama, *op. cit.*, 314; several other names in Roschini, *op. cit.*, 92.
[210] C. Mazzella, S.J., *De Deo creante praelectiones scholastico-dogmaticae*, 2nd ed. (Rome, 1880), 814–821; L. Janssens, O.S.B., *Summa theologica*, 5; *Tractatus de Deo-Homine* (Freiburg, 1902), 34–40; Roschini, *op. cit.*, 95–96. Cf. likewise, for the same opinion, M. Llamera, O.P., *El problema del débito y la redención preservatica de María*, in EM, 15 (1955), 169–223.

cipally within the Franciscan School, was quite common among theologians during the 17th and 18th centuries, and has found not a few adherents in modern times, such as Longpré, Bonnefoy, García Garcés, Alonso, Wolter, Carr, Philips, and many others.[211]

It is generally admitted that the first two opinions mentioned above sufficiently safeguard the truth that Mary was redeemed by the merits of Christ; although at times this is done at the expense of her unparalleled holiness.[212] As to the third view, which is the one we favor, many theologians feel that it is untenable for these

[211] E. Longpré, O.F.M., *L'Assomption et l'école franciscaine,* in *SM,* 4, 209; Bonnefoy, *Quelques théories modernes du "debitum peccati,"* in *EphM,* 4 (1954), 269–331; N. García Garcés, C.M.F., *¿Debió tener la Santísima Virgen el pecado original?,* in *EphM,* 5 (1955), 95–110; J. Alonso, C.M.F., *De quolibet debito a B. M. Virgine prorsus excludendo,* ibid., 4 (1954), 201–242; id, *Num B. Virgo peccati debito fuerit obnoxia,* ibid., 5 (1955), 33–46; A. Wolter, *art. cit.,* 62–70; A. Carr, O.F.M.Conv., *Mary's Immaculate Conception,* in *Mariology* (Carol), 1, 379–386; G. Philips, *Quelques réflexions sur les présupposés du "debitum peccati" de la sainte Vierge,* in *EphM,* 5 (1955), 87–93. Cf. also Crisóstomo de Pamplona, O.F.M.Cap., *La redención preservativa de María y el requisito esencial de la preservación,* in *EM,* 15 (1955), 153–167.

[212] Thus, for example, in his desperate effort to harmonize the teaching of St. Thomas with that of Pius IX, N. del Prado, O.P., does not hesitate to declare—sixty-five years *after* the papal definition!— that Mary's "total preservation from original sin seems to be contrary to Catholic faith" (in *Divus Thomas et Bulla dogmatica "Ineffabilis Deus,"* Fribourg, 1919, 119). It is interesting to note that the premises which led Father del Prado to this incredible conclusion were precisely the theories of those who insist that Our Lady contracted a real debt of sin. Though his conclusion is diametrically opposed to the teaching of Pius IX, nevertheless, we must credit the author with being perfectly logical and consistent. Similarly, Fr. C. Friethoff, O.P., believes that, since Mary incurred the debt of original sin, it is perfectly correct to say, even now, that she "contracted" (!) that sin. (Cf. *Quomodo caro B. V. M. in originali concepta fuerit,* in *Ang,* 10, 1933, 327.)

reasons: (1) it does not take into account the fact that Mary was a true child of Adam by way of ordinary generation; (2) it withdraws her from the influence of Christ's Redemption, for if she had never incurred at least a remote necessity to contract original sin, the redeeming grace of the Savior could hardly be said to have "preserved" her from that sin.

To these observations the exponents of the third theory answer:

(a) By itself, ordinary generation from Adam is not sufficient to create in the offspring a *necessity* to contract original sin. It merely gives rise to a *possibility* of contracting it. As such, it constitutes the loss of one title to grace in the present order of things. For a person to be involved in the sin of Adam a second factor is necessary, namely, a decree of God withdrawing His grace from that individual whose solidarity with Adam in the supernatural order has been foreseen. In other words, the debt of sin presupposes that a person depends both on the physical *and moral* headship of our first parent.[213] Now, Adam was not the moral head of Our Lady; she did not depend on him for her grace. Before Mary was predestined to be a child of Adam, she had already been chosen as the worthy Mother of God and was thus the object of a special divine predilection. Therefore, if owing to Adam's sin, Our Lady lost *one* title to grace,

[213] Cf. N. García Garcés, *Sesión académica inmaculista en la Gregoriana*, in *EphM*, 4 (1954), 360.

she still retained her previous and far greater title to grace arising from her predestination to the divine Motherhood. Surely this latter title more than neutralizes any possibility of sin induced by the fact that she would receive her physical nature from Adam.[214]

(b) The third theory not only does not withdraw Our Lady from the salutary influence of the Redemption, but it makes her all the more indebted to it. The efficacy of Christ's redemptive grace was so overwhelming in her case that it not only preserved her from the actual contraction of sin, but even placed her *beyond the reach of the law of sin*. In the order of God's intention, Our Lady's original grace was foreseen with a logical priority to the Redemption. However, in the order of execution, God decreed that the conferring of this grace would be merited for her by the Savior's Passion and Death.[215] Hence it remains true, even in this third theory, that Mary was truly "redeemed" by Christ. Granted that the word "redeemed," as used here, is taken in a less strict sense than when applied to us. But this does in no way detract from Christ's redemptive role. On the contrary, as the concept of "redemption" loses some of its strict connotation, it also gains in sublimity and perfection,

214 Cf. A. Wolter, *art. cit.*, esp. 68.

215 This explanation is in harmony with our views relative to Mary's predestination as propounded elsewhere (Part 1, Ch. 1). For the theory of Mary's freedom from the debt of sin, based on *non*-Scotistic principles, cf. the excellent article by Father Basilio de San Pablo, C.P., *Impresiones de un independiente sobre la cuestión del débito*, in EphM, 5 (1955), 9–32.

thus redounding to the greater glory of the Savior. In this sense Pius IX declared that Our Lady was "redeemed in a *more sublime* way," and more recently Pius XII stated that she had been "redeemed in the *most perfect* manner."[216]

(c) In confirmation of this view we may appeal to the teaching of the apostolic constitution *Ineffabilis Deus.* In it Pius IX clearly affirms that Our Blessed Lady was "NEVER affected by (or exposed to) the law of the curse";[217] that she was always purer and holier than the very angels.[218] Surely the angels were never involved in the sin of Adam, either proximately or remotely. Therefore, neither was the Queen of Angels. According to the Pope, Mary was far holier than Eve when the latter was still in the state of original justice.[219] If so, are we not to infer that the Mother of God, the *"parentum reparatrix,"*[220] was farther removed from the original curse than the mother of the living according to the flesh? The Holy Father likewise reminds us that Our Lady was predestined "in one and the same decree" with Christ, and before all creatures.[221] Hence Mary belongs, first and

---

[216] Pius IX, *Ineffabilis Deus,* in ADSC, 6, 839; Pius XII, *Fulgens corona,* in AAS, 45 (1953), 591. On the specific meaning of "redemption" as applied to Mary, cf. Pedro de Alcántara (Martínez), O.F.M., *Duns Escoto y la bula "Ineffabilis,"* in EM, 13 (1953), 309–331; id., *La redención preservativa de María,* in EphM, 4 (1954), 243–267; id., *La redención y el débito de María,* in VyV, 12 (1954), 1–48; 445–480; Bonnefoy, *art. cit.,* in EphM, 4 (1954), 307–314.

[217] ADSC, 6, 840.

[218] *Ibid.,* 6, 841.

[219] *Ibid.,* 6, 840.

[220] *Ibid.*

[221] *Ibid.,* 6, 836.

foremost, to the orbit of Christ, not to that of Adam. Furthermore, as the Pope emphasizes, Mary always shared most intimately the Savior's *absolute* triumph over sin.[222] Therefore, if she enters the orbit of Adam at all, it is in order to destroy his sin, not in order to be affected by it, either proximately or remotely.

In view of the above, the Immaculate Conception means that Our Lady was preserved, not from a sin she *should* have contracted (as one frequently reads), but rather from a sin she *would* have contracted, had God so decided. But, as a matter of fact, God did not so decide. Therefore, her involvement in the law of sin ought to be relegated to the realm of purely unrealized hypotheses, concerning which divine revelation is utterly silent.[223]

The argument is further corroborated by the following observation: If God had from all eternity subjected Mary to the law of sin (that is exactly what a real *debitum* implies), and then, in the first instant of her conception, decided to suspend the actual application of that law, He would have thereby reversed or annulled His previous decree. This, of course, is impossible because of His immutability.[224]

[222] *Ibid.*, 6, 839. Cf. our extended commentary in *De Corredemptione* . . . (Vatican City, 1950), 113–121.

[223] Cf. Carol, *Our Lady's Immunity from the Debt of Sin*, in *MS*, 6 (1955), 164–168.

[224] Cf. Bonnefoy, *art. cit.*, in *EphM*, 4 (1954), 328–329.

Appendix II

Mary's Immunity from Concupiscence

Concupiscence is an inclination toward a sensible good against or prior to the dictates of right reason. It may be considered as a habit, or as the exercise of it, namely, inordinate movements. While strictly speaking concupiscence in itself is not formally sinful, nevertheless, in the present order, it involves a certain moral taint, inasmuch as it springs from original sin and leads to personal sin.[225]

It is the unanimous teaching of Catholic theologians that Our Lady was always immune from all inordinate movements. This thesis is regarded as at least "theologically certain," although some authors go further and consider it "implicitly defined" in the bull *Ineffabilis Deus* of Pius IX.[226]

In the Middle Ages quite a few theologians, following St. Thomas,[227] taught that Our Lady was subject to the *habit* of concupiscence, but that it was held in check, as it were, until the time of the Incarnation when she was completely freed from it. The Franciscans, on the contrary, and those who shared their views on the Immaculate Conception, consistently claimed that concupiscence had been radically and totally destroyed in Mary from

---

[225] Conc. Trid., sessio 5; DB, 792. Cf. Carr, *art. cit.*, 386–391.
[226] For example, L. Janssens, O.S.B., *Summa Theologica*, 5: *De Deo-Homine* (Freiburg, 1902), 41.
[227] *Summa Theologica*, III, 27, 4, ad 3.

the very first moment of her existence. In other words, Mary was *never* subject to concupiscence. They rightly argued that this immunity was logically demanded by her exalted dignity and her unparalleled purity.[228] This view was soon endorsed by many other theologians and eventually (particularly after the definition of the Immaculate Conception) accepted by all.

[228] Cf. Jerome de Montefortino, O.F.M., *Ven. J. Duns Scoti Summa Theologica*, 5 (Rome, 1903), 302–304. On the various views relative to concupiscence in Our Lady, cf. Roschini, *op. cit.*, 96 ff.; cf. likewise A. Van Hove, *De immunitate B. M. Virginis a concupiscentia*, in CM, 14 (1940), 36–42, where he defends the view that immunity from concupiscence is not necessarily connected with immunity from original sin.

CHAPTER TWO

Our Lady's Fullness of Grace

THE privilege of the Immaculate Conception may be regarded as a *negative* sanctity inasmuch as it bears direct reference to immunity from original sin. However, in the present order of things, the absence of sin in the soul necessarily implies the presence of grace (*positive* sanctity); hence, after treating of the former, we must now consider the latter.[229]

By "grace" here is meant the whole organism which enables a person to act supernaturally, namely: sanctifying grace, the infused virtues, and the gifts of the Holy Ghost. By "fullness" of grace we mean, not the absolute fullness which is incapable of increase, but a relative one denoting the overwhelming abundance of supernatural endowments proportionate to the unique dignity of God's Mother. We shall discuss briefly the following points: (1) Mary's initial grace; and (2) its increase throughout her life.

[229] On this subject, cf. G. Frénaud, O.S.B., *La grâce de l'Immaculée Conception*, in VIIe *Congrès Marial National. L'Immaculée Conception* (Lyons, 1955), 221–249; B. Ravagnan, *De augmento gratiae initialis in B. M. Virgine*, in Mm, 3 (1941), 269–285; id., *De Mariae plenitudine gratiae*, in Mm, 3 (1941), 102–124; 4 (1942), 42–56.

122

Article 1

MARY'S INITIAL GRACE

That Our Blessed Lady was endowed by God with a fullness of grace at least from the time of the Annunciation cannot be called into question, since this is clearly attested to by the angel's greeting (Luke 1, 28) as understood by Tradition and the magisterium. Furthermore, that she enjoyed a fullness of grace from the very first instant of her conception is held by all Catholic theologians as certain. The reason is that Mary was predestined to be the worthy Mother of God, and this dignity postulated a fitting preparation in her from the first moment of her existence.

Nevertheless, ever since the 16th century, theologians began to establish a comparison between Our Lady's grace and that of other creatures, and it is here that their views do not always coincide. Their teaching on the matter may be summarized in the four following propositions:

I. Our Lady's *initial grace* (that is, the grace she received at the moment of her conception) was greater than the *initial* grace of any saint or angel taken singly. This is admitted by all.

II. Our Lady's *initial* grace was greater than the *final* grace of any saint or angel taken singly. This, too, is generally admitted by theologians.[230]

III. Our Lady's *initial* grace was greater than the *initial*

[230] Cf. Keuppens, *op. cit.*, 41–42.

grace of all the saints and angels taken collectively. This thesis is solidly probable, and is also held by the majority of theologians.

IV. Our Lady's *initial* grace was greater than the *final* grace of all the saints and angels taken *collectively*. This thesis has been vigorously defended by the Franciscans since the beginning of the controversy, and has won the support of a great many theologians. It is rejected by Raynaud, Cardinal Lépicier, Baudiment and others.[231]

The arguments in favor of this theory may be grouped under these two headings: (A) the magisterium of the Church, and (B) theological reason.

A. *The Magisterium of the Church.* Pope Pius IX in his bull *Ineffabilis Deus* states: "From the beginning and before the ages God chose and appointed a Mother for His Only-Begotten Son . . . and on her He showered so much love, with preference to all other creatures, that only in her case was He pleased with a most loving complacency. He, therefore, enriched her with an abundance of all heavenly gifts drawn from the treasury of the divinity, far more than all the angelic spirits and all the saints, in such a wonderful manner that she . . . all beautiful and perfect, might display a fullness of holiness *greater than which none is at all conceivable under God,*

---

[231] Cf. Th. Raynaud, *Diptycha Mariana* (Lyons, 1665), 159; Lépicier, *op. cit.*, 230–235; L. Baudiment, *De quelques outrance de la théologie mariale contemporaine*, in *ATh*, 6 (1943), 105–115. The last author was answered by P. E. Vadeboncoeur, C.SS.R., in *Quelle est cette outrance? La Pleine de grâce*, in *RUO*, 16 (1946), 209*–226*. For the many authorities favoring this doctrine, cf. F. X. Godts, C.SS.R., *La sainteté initiale de l'Immaculée* (Brussels, 1904); Keuppens, *op. cit.*, 42; Roschini, *op. cit.*, 129; de Aldama, *op. cit.*, 324.

and which no one, with the exception of God, can even grasp."[232] Practically the same thing is taught by Pope Leo XIII in his encyclical *Magna Dei Matris*[233] and by Pius XII in his *Mystici Corporis*.[234]

B. *Theological Reason*. The thesis is based on the truth that the grace bestowed upon any person is always commensurate with that person's dignity or office. Hence, Our Lady's fullness of grace must be measured by the standard of her unparalleled dignity as Mother of God and Queen of all creation.

Besides, grace is the effect of God's love toward a soul. In other words, a soul is endowed with grace in direct proportion to the intensity of God's love. Now, it is logical to suppose that, since God had predestined Mary to be the worthy Mother of His Son, He loved her from the very beginning with an incomparable love, with a love that was far greater than the love He bestowed on all the saints and angels taken collectively.

Furthermore, as Coredemptrix, Spiritual Mother, Mediatrix and Queen of all creation, Our Lady was, with Christ and under Him, like a fountain from which grace was to be derived for all her children and subjects. Hence, it stands to reason that she should have, even from the beginning, more grace than all rational creatures put together.[235]

[232] ADSC, 6, 536.
[233] ASS, 25 (1892), 141.
[234] AAS, 35 (1943), 247.
[235] Cf. Bover, *Santidad inicial de María*, in EE, 28 (1954), 563–580, esp. 566–571.

Article 2

MARY'S INCREASE IN GRACE

As mentioned above, the fullness of grace Our Lady received in the very first instant of her conception was only relative, not absolute. In other words, it was capable of increase. In this connection theologians are wont to discuss three questions in particular:

I. the time when Our Lady began to merit an increase of grace;

II. the means by which she caused that increase;

III. the continuity of that growth.

I. Did Our Lady begin to merit an increase of grace from the very first instant of her conception? This could be possible only in the hypothesis that she enjoyed the use of reason from that moment. Here theologians are divided. Some openly deny that she did.[236] Others believe that she had the use of reason necessary for merit, but only in the first moment of her conception.[237] Finally, the greater number contend that she possessed this exceptional privilege permanently from the very beginning.[238] This third opinion seems acceptable for the following reasons:

[236] *Summa Theologica*, III, 27, 3; I. Gerson, *De susceptione humanitatis Christi*, ver. 20; *opera omnia*, 1 (Antwerp, 1706), 453; Pohle-Preuss, *op. cit.*, 30–31; cf. A. Martinelli, O.F.M., *De primo instanti Conceptionis B. M. Virginis; disquisitio de usu rationis* (Rome, 1950), 27–31.

[237] V. Contenson, O.P., *Theologia mentis et cordis*, lib. 10, diss. 6, cap. 1, spec. 2 (ed. Paris, 1875), 3, 265; Lépicier, *op. cit.*, 223–227; E. Campana, *Maria nel dogma cattolico*, 4th ed. (Turin-Rome, 1936), 396.

[238] Cf. the impressive number of authors mentioned by Martinelli, *op. cit.*, esp. 16–19; 31–59; Aldama, *op. cit.*, 326.

A. It was more noble and fitting for Our Lady to be sanctified in the womb of her mother after the manner of an adult (namely, by eliciting an act of her free will and thus consciously cooperating with divine grace), than after the manner of infants who are unable to prepare themselves for the reception of grace.

B. If Mary had been deprived of the use of reason immediately after her original sanctification, she would have been less perfect from that moment on, since she would be incapable of human acts. In this hypothesis the unique supernatural organism which God lavished upon her from the beginning would have remained sterile, its normal fecundity being unreasonably hampered.

II. As to the means by which Our Lady increased in grace, we must mention, first of all, the wonderful dispositions of her soul which sanctified everything she did. If the just man merits an increase of grace by performing good deeds, with far greater reason must the same be said of Our Lady whose every action was saturated with the purest love of God. Since she was completely free from concupiscence and all imperfections, there was nothing to tarnish the purity of her intention and thus retard the progress of her supernatural life.[239]

Another factor which contributed to Mary's growth in holiness later on in life, was the fruitful reception of the sacraments. Obviously, she did not, and could not, receive all the seven sacraments. Not Penance, because of her

[239] Cf. E. Neubert, S.M., *Mary in Doctrine* (Milwaukee, Wis., 1954), 227–228.

immunity from all sin; not Holy Orders, because of her sex; not Matrimony, because when she married St. Joseph the marriage contract had not as yet been raised to the dignity of a sacrament, and St. Joseph most likely died before this took place; not Extreme Unction, because in order to receive this sacrament a person must be in danger of death arising from illness, which was impossible in Our Lady. Besides, the proper effect of Extreme Unction is to remit sin or at least the remains of sin in the soul, and Our Lady had neither.

As to the Holy Eucharist, we may be sure that Our Lady received it, and perhaps even daily, as was customary among the early Christians (Acts 2:46), whom she certainly exceeded in fervor and love of Christ. This was unquestionably the greatest source of her merit and growth in sanctity. With regard to Baptism, we may be equally sure that Our Lady willingly submitted to it, most likely with the other disciples before the Last Supper. This she did, not in order to be cleansed from original sin, which she never had, but in order to be marked with the sacramental character, to be officially incorporated into the Church, and to be able to approach the other sacraments of which she was capable. As to Confirmation, it is reasonably held by theologians that she received it in a more eminent manner than we, when her soul was flooded with the plenitude of the Holy Spirit and His Gifts on Pentecost day (Acts 1:14).[240]

III. Did Our Lady merit an increase of grace continu-

[240] Cf. Roschini, *op. cit.*, 140–146.

ously and by everything she did during the course of her entire life? It is generally admitted as certain that she did. In fact, many theologians, including some Doctors of the Church, have advanced the opinion that her merit was uninterrupted even by sleep.[241] Others, however, would hesitate to go that far.[242]

Scholion I. As mentioned before, together with sanctifying grace Our Lady received also the theological and moral virtues, and the gifts of the Holy Ghost. The former made it possible for her to posit supernaturally meritorious acts; the latter aided her to perform these meritorious acts more perfectly and more in accordance with the inspirations of the Holy Spirit. That Our Lady practised all virtues in a most excellent manner at all times is a thesis now universally received among Catholic theologians.[243] The very pages of Sacred Scripture give us a sufficiently clear glimpse of her unshaken faith (Luke 1:45), of her prompt obedience (Luke 2:6; 2:22), and of her profound humility (Luke 1:38, 48).[244] However, since Our Lady was entirely free from concupiscence, she did not have the virtue of continence which

[241] Cf. Aldama, *op. cit.*, 326; Roschini, *op. cit.*, 138–139.

[242] Cf. G. Van Noort, *Tractatus de Deo Redemptore*, 4th ed. (Hillversum in Holland, 1925), 167, footnote 5; B. H. Merkelbach, O.P., *Mariologia* (Paris, 1939), 212.

[243] Cf. E. Dublanchy, S.M., art. *Marie*, in *DTC*, 9, 2425–2428; Neubert, *op. cit.*, 202–224; Garrigou-Lagrange, *op. cit.*, 149–154; Keuppens, *op. cit.*, 49–52; Merkelbach, *op. cit.*, 183–196; Roschini, *op. cit.*, 148–182; Elías de la Dolorosa, C.P., *Virtudes y dones del Espíritu Santo en la Santísima Virgen*, in *EM*, 5 (1946), 205–248.

[244] Cf. the interesting interpretations of this text with reference to Mary's humility in E. A. Ryan, S.J., *Historical Notes on Luke 1:48*, in *MS*, 3 (1952), 228–235.

helps us to resist our unruly passions. Nor, again, could she practise the virtue of penance. Being absolutely free from all sin and even the slightest imperfections, she could not experience any sorrow for them. The intense sorrow she experienced for *our* sins was related to the virtue of charity, not penance. It is disputed among theologians whether or not she had the latter virtue only as a *habit*. In our opinion, the question should be answered in the negative.[245]

Scholion II. Other interesting questions discussed by theologians relative to Mary's grace, are: (A) whether it shared the nature of Christ's *capital* grace; (B) whether it differs from ours not only in degree and perfection, but also ontologically; (C) whether it had the same nature and characteristics as the original justice given to Adam and Eve in paradise. Here we shall but summarize the various opinions on the matter. The first question is answered in the affirmative by Fernández, Bello, Bover, Keuppens, and many others; and in the negative by García Garcés and Roschini.[245a] As to the second question, Alonso and Bover favor an ontological difference, while Roschini is against it.[245b] The answer to the third

---

[245] For the opposite opinion, cf. Merkelbach, *op. cit.*, 190.

[245a] A. Fernández, O.P., *De Mediatione Beatae Virginis secundum doctrinam D. Thomae*, in CT, 38 (1928), 152–158; L. M. Bello, O.F.M., *De B. Maria Virgine omnium gratiarum Mediatrice* (Rome, 1938), 22–28; Bover, *art. cit.*, 575–577; Keuppens, *op. cit.*, 53–55; N. García Garcés, *Mater Corredemptrix* (Rome, 1940), 283–297; Roschini, *op. cit.*, 352–357.

[245b] J. M. Alonso, *Naturaleza y fundamentos de la gracia de la Virgen*, in EM, 5 (1946), 11–110; Bover, *art. cit.*, 577–578; Roschini, *op. cit.*, 146–148.

question naturally depends on whether or not one holds that Our Lady was constituted in the state of original justice in the first moment of her conception. One group contends that she was, although *de facto* she freely renounced the gifts of impassibility and immortality connected with that state.[245c] A second group maintains that Mary never enjoyed the state of original justice. They claim, of course, that she was free from sin and concupiscence, but the gifts of immortality and impassibility were lost by Adam for all his descendants, regardless of whether or not they contracted original sin.[245d]

In our opinion, Our Lady's grace had nothing to do with the state of original justice as enjoyed by our first parents, in the sense that it was entirely independent of it.[245e] She was not "deprived" of impassibility and immortality. She lacked these gifts, not because Adam lost them for all his descendants (Our Lady *lost* NOTH-ING in Adam!), but simply because God had decreed from all eternity to give her a human body (intrinsically mortal regardless of sin) so that she might fulfill her office as Coredemptrix of the human race.

[245c] Lépicier, *op. cit.*, ed. 5, 358–361; Janssens, *op. cit.*, 864. In the opinion of Roschini, *op. cit.*, 221–223, Mary renounced only the gift of impassibility, not of immortality.

[245d] A. Gorrino, *Maria Santissima, Madre di Dio e Madre nostra* (Turin, 1938), 60–61; G. Alastruey, *Tratado de la Virgen Santísima,* 3rd ed. (Madrid, 1952), 403–404. On this whole question, cf. Carr, *art. cit.*, 391–394.

[245e] Cf. Bonnefoy, *L'Assomption de la Très Sainte Vierge et sa prédestination,* in SM, 4 (Montreal, 1948), 321.

SECTION TWO

*Prerogatives Conferred on Mary during
the Course of Her Life*

The most important prerogatives conferred on Our Blessed Lady during the course of her life were: perfect immunity from all actual sin; perpetual virginity of body and soul; and a unique intellectual endowment. We shall now treat of these in three separate chapters.

Mary's Immunity from Actual Sin

THE matter to be discussed in this chapter may be conveniently divided into the following sections: statement and explanation of the Catholic thesis; errors in this connection; proofs of the doctrine from the magisterium, Sacred Scripture, Tradition, and theological reason.

I. *Catholic Thesis:* The Blessed Virgin Mary, by a unique privilege of God, was preserved free from all actual sin during the entire course of her life. The meaning of this Catholic thesis is that Our Lady was never guilty of personal sin, either mortal or venial; that she was immune even from the slightest moral imperfections or wilful violation or omission of any counsel of God or her superiors. Mary owes this privilege, not to her own merits, but to a singular favor of God.[246]

II. *Errors:* The thesis of Mary's sinlessness was vigorously denied by Luther, Calvin, and the Protestants in general, with the possible exception of some Episcopalians.[247] Strangely enough, some Fathers and ecclesiastical writers in the first five centuries made occasional statements which are definitely at variance with the

[246] Cf. M. J. Scheeben, *Mariology*, transl. Geukers, 2 (St. Louis, Mo., 1947), 112–139.

[247] An excellent and lengthy refutation of non-Catholic attacks on Mary's sinlessness may be found in St. Peter Canisius, *De Maria Virgine incomparabili et Dei Genitrice sacrosancta*, lib. 4; in *Summa aurea de laudibus B. V. Mariae*, ed. J. Bourassé, 8 (Paris, 1862), 1194–1450.

traditional Catholic position in this matter. For example, St. Basil of Caesarea (d. 379) was of the opinion that, at the foot of the Cross, Our Lady was troubled with doubts concerning the divinity of her Son.[248] This error, dating back to Origen (d. 254/255), was endorsed later on by St. Cyril of Alexandria (d. 444), the vigorous champion of Mary's divine Maternity against Nestorius.[249] St. John Chrysostom (d. 404) was not less unorthodox when he claimed that Mary's request for a miracle at the marriage feast of Cana was actually prompted by vainglory.[250]

III. *Proofs of the Catholic Doctrine.*

A. *The Magisterium of the Church.* In the year 1547 the Council of Trent made the following pronouncement: "If anyone shall say that man, after he is once justified, can avoid throughout his lifetime all sin, even venial, except by a special privilege of God, *as the Church holds concerning the Blessed Virgin*, let him be anathema."[251] In view of this conciliar declaration, the

---

[248] St. Basil, *Epist.* 260, *ad Optimum; PG*, 32, 965–968.

[249] Origen, *Hom. 17 in Lucam; PG*, 13, 1845; St. Cyril, *Comm. in Joannis evangelium*, lib. 12; *PG*, 74, 661–664. Cf. G. Jouassard, *L'interprétation par saint Cyrille d'Alexandrie de la scène de Marie au pied de la croix*, in VgI, 4 (Rome, 1955), 28–47.

[250] St. John Chrysostom, *Hom. 21 in Joannem*, n. 2; *PG*, 59, 130. A very fine and objective commentary on these and similar patristic passages may be found in Burghardt, *Mary in Eastern Patristic Thought*, in *Mariology* (Carol), 2, Ch. 3. Cf. also Card. Newman's answer to Dr. Pusey, published under the title *Mary the Mother of Jesus* (New York, s.a.), 121–137.

[251] DB, 833.

thesis that Mary was always free from personal sin must be considered *de fide*, i.e., an article of our faith. Some theologians, however, disagree with this qualification and refer to the thesis as merely *"doctrina catholica"*[252] or *"proxima fidei,"*[253] or finally *"theologice certa."*[254] This is not enough. The circumstances accompanying the drafting of that particular canon clearly indicate that the Council meant to define the doctrine as an article of our faith.[255]

Again, in 1567, Pope Pius V proclaimed Our Lady's immunity from personal sin by condemning one of Baius' propositions to the contrary.[256] In 1854 Pius IX declared that Mary "was *always* free from *absolutely all* stain of sin."[257] This coincides with the unqualified statement of Pius XII in his encyclical *Mystici Corporis* (1943) to the effect that Our Lady "was free from both *personal* and hereditary sin, and always most closely united with her Son."[258]

B. *Argument from Sacred Scripture.* In the Proto-evangelium (Genesis 3:15) we are told that Almighty God Himself placed a *perpetual* and *absolute* enmity between the devil and Mary. An enmity of this nature

[252] For example, Merkelbach, *op. cit.*, 142.

[253] L. Lercher, S.J., *Institutiones Theologiae Dogmaticae*, 5th ed., 3 (Barcelona, 1951), 315.

[254] I. Mendive, *Institutiones Theologiae Dogmaticae-Scholasticae*, 3 (Vallisoleti, 1895), n. 311 f.

[255] Cf. Aldama, *El valor dogmático de la doctrina sobre la inmunidad de pecado venial en Nuestra Señora*, in ATG, 9 (1946), 53–67, esp. 58–60.

[256] DB, 1073.

[257] ADSC, 6, 836.

[258] AAS, 35 (1943), 247.

necessarily excludes original and mortal sin. Does it exclude also venial sin? We know that venial sin does not destroy sanctifying grace (the friendship of God) in the soul; nevertheless, because it connotes a positive moral evil, it is quite incompatible with the absolute holiness which the Protoevangelium postulates for Our Blessed Lady.

C. *Argument from Tradition.* The Tradition in connection with Mary's freedom from actual sin may be divided into the following stages: (1) from the 1st to the 5th century; (2) from the 5th to the 13th century; and (3) from the 13th century to our day.

(1) *From the First to the Fifth Century.* Many of the early Fathers and ecclesiastical writers taught Mary's sinlessness *implicitly*, i.e., by frequently referring to her as the Woman who, together with her Son, would destroy the dominion of Satan, and hence of sin. Others are more explicit on the point. For example, St. Ephraem (d. 373) thus addressed Our Lord: "Thou and Thy Mother are the only ones who are immune from all stain; for there is no spot in Thee, O Lord, nor any taint in Thy Mother."[259] And St. Ambrose (d. 397): "Through grace the Virgin was free from all stain of sin."[260] Some of the early writers, however, were not logical in their teaching concerning Mary, for in a few

[259] St. Ephraem, *Sermones exegetici; op. omn. syr. et lat.*, 2 (Rome, 1740), 327.
[260] St. Ambrose, *Exposit. in Ps. 118*, serm. 22, n. 30; PL, 15, 1599 (ed. 1866).

instances they attribute some imperfections to her, as we have seen above.

(2) *From the Fifth to the Thirteenth.* In this second period Our Lady's sinlessness is never called into question, but is rather taken for granted by all. St. Augustine (d. 430) may be said to represent the general attitude of his time, at least in the Western world, when he pens the well-known text: "We must except the Holy Virgin Mary, concerning whom—out of respect for the Lord—I wish to raise no question when dealing with sin."[261] Our Lady's sinlessness is likewise explicity emphasized by Paschasius Radbertus (d. 860), Eadmerus of Canterbury (d. 1124), Hildebert of Mans (d. 1133), St. Bernard (d. 1153), Richard of St. Victor (d. 1173), Walter of St. Victor (d. 1180) and many others.[262]

(3) *From the Thirteenth Century to the Present Time.* In the 13th century the Scholastics not only taught that Mary had always been free from all actual or personal sin (whether mortal or venial), but they also began to discuss the causes—proximate and remote—of that sinlessness. This obviously led them to consider

[261] St. Augustine, *De natura et gratia,* cap. 36, n. 42; *PL,* 44, 267.
[262] Paschasius Radbertus, *De partu Virginis,* lib. 1; *PL,* 120, 1371; Eadmer of Canterbury, *De excellentia B. Virginis,* cap. 2; *PL,* 159, 560; Hildebert of Mans, *Serm.* 69; *PL,* 181, 677; St. Bernard, *Epist.* 184, n. 5; *PL,* 183, 420; Richard of St. Victor, *Expl. in Cant. Canticorum,* 26, 29; *PL,* 482, 516; Walter of St. Victor, *Excerpta ex libris contra quatuor labyrinthos Franciae*; PL, 119, 1154. Cf. Dublanchy, *art. cit.,* in *DTC,* 9, 2414–2416. For an explanation of the Scriptural difficulties raised against the thesis, cf. S. Bonano, C.M.F., *Mary's Immunity from Actual Sin,* in *Mariology* (Carol), 1, 400–405.

the question of Our Lady's *impeccability* or inability to sin.

There are two types of impeccability: metaphysical and moral. The former is predicated exclusively of God who is holiness itself, and also of Christ, due to the Hypostatic Union. The latter belongs to the angels and saints on account of the beatific vision, and likewise to Our Blessed Lady, although for reasons other than those mentioned in the case of God, Christ, the angels and saints.

According to Alexander of Hales (d. 1245), Mary was impeccable because of her fullness of grace.[263] According to St. Bonaventure (d. 1274), Mary received a special divine assistance which strengthened the potencies of her soul, and this made it impossible for her to sin.[264] St. Thomas (d. 1274) thought that Mary was impeccable owing to a constant act of divine Providence removing all occasions of sin from her path.[265] Finally, in the opinion of Suárez (d. 1617) and most theologians, the remote cause of Mary's impeccability was the divine Motherhood; the proximate cause was threefold: the lack of concupiscence, the fullness of grace and an act of divine Providence which not only removed

---

[263] Alexander of Hales, *Summa Theologica*, lib. 3, *De Verbo Incarnato*, tr. 2, q. 2, memb. 3, cap. 2, art. 2 (ed. Quaracchi, 1948), 4, 124.

[264] St. Bonaventure, *In 3 Sent.*, dist. 3, pars 1, art. 1, q. 3 (ed. Quarachi, 1887), 3, 77–78 (Mary was impeccable "propter potentiae confirmationem et defectus ablationem").

[265] St. Thomas, *Contra Gentiles*, lib. 3, cap. 155. Cf. Bonano, *art. cit.*, 407.

all occasions of sin from her but also confirmed her in grace.[266]

D. *Argument from Reason.* There are three theological reasons in particular which demand Mary's absolute sinlessness: (1) her divine Motherhood; (2) her role as Coredemptrix; (3) her dignity as universal Queen.

(1) Mary was predestined from all eternity to be the *worthy* Mother of God. Any guilt of personal sin in her soul would naturally render her unworthy of so sublime a prerogative, for the shame of a parent redounds to the disgrace of the child.

(2) Mary was chosen by God to be the Coredemptrix of mankind. And, as St. Bonaventure explains, "it is fitting that the Blessed Virgin, through whom the shame of sin was taken away, should so overcome the devil as never to be his victim."[267]

(3) Mary was and is the Queen of all creation. But how could the Queen require her subjects to observe the laws of God if she herself had failed therein?

Therefore, we must assume that, since God had freely chosen Mary for all the above offices, He owed it to Himself to bestow the grace of sinlessness and impeccability upon her soul.

[266] Suárez, *De mysteriis vitae Christi*, disp. 4, sect. 4; cf. Aldama, *op. cit.*, 321.
[267] St. Bonaventure, *In 3 Sent.*, pars 1, art. 2, q. 1, in corp.; *opera omnia*, 3, 73.

Mary's Perpetual Virginity

THE term "virgin" may be used in various senses. It may mean an unmarried woman, or a person (man or woman) who has not had sexual intercourse. Again, it may be applied to things unused or unsullied, as when we speak of a "virgin field" or the "virgin snow." Virginity, or the state of being a virgin, when applied to persons, may be either internal or external. Internal virginity is a virtue which consists in a firm purpose of avoiding all venereal delectation, even though licit (as in legitimate marriage). External or bodily virginity refers to the natural condition of physiological integrity with which we are born into the world. It is lost either by sexual intercourse (whether sinful or licit), by the sin of pollution, or finally, in the case of women, by some natural or accidental act causing the breaking of the hymen.

At present we are concerned with Our Lady's external or bodily virginity, the treatment of which we shall divide into three sections: virginity *before* the birth of Christ; virginity *during* the birth of Christ; and virginity *after* the birth of Christ. Our Lady's internal virginity will be touched upon in a scholion.

General Thesis: Mary was always a virgin: before, during and after the birth of Christ. This thesis was defined as an article of our faith by the Lateran Council in the year 649 under Pope St. Martin I, with these words: "If anyone does not, in accord with the holy Fathers, acknowledge the holy, *ever virgin* and immaculate Mary as really and truly the Mother of God, inasmuch as she, in the fullness of time, and without seed, conceived by the Holy Spirit of God the Word Himself, who before all time was born of God the Father, and without loss of integrity brought Him forth, and after His birth preserved her virginity inviolate, let him be condemned."[268]

Let us now take up the three parts of this thesis separately, indicating the errors in its connection, the various arguments in its favor, and the objections advanced by the heretics.

I. *Mary Was a Virgin before the Birth of Christ.*

A. *Meaning of the Thesis.* The teaching of the Catholic Church is that Mary was a virgin up to the time of the Annunciation, and that she conceived Christ by the supernatural aid of the Holy Ghost, and not through the aid of St. Joseph or any other man.

B. *Errors.* This Catholic truth was denied:

(1) in the middle of the second century by the Jews who claimed that Christ was the offspring of an adulterous union;

(2) by the ancient sects of the Ebionites and Gnostics

[268] DB, 256.

who taught that Christ had been conceived in the ordinary and normal way by Mary and Joseph;

(3) by the Anabaptists (16th century) and by many
Protestants and Rationalists who reject the very possibility of parthenogenesis.[269]

C. *Proofs of the Thesis.* The Catholic teaching concerning Our Lady's virginity before the birth of Christ
has the support of the magisterium, of Sacred Scripture
and of Tradition.

(1) *The Magisterium.* The magisterium has, from the
beginning, constantly, clearly and emphatically taught
Mary's virginity before the birth of Christ. For example,
the Apostles' Creed states, speaking of Christ: "who was
conceived by the Holy Ghost, born of the Virgin
Mary."[270] The same truth is found in the Creed or
Symbol of Nicea[271] and in the canons of many Church
Councils.[272]

(2) *Sacred Scripture.* In the book of the prophet
Isaias (7, 14) we read: "Behold a virgin shall conceive
and bear a son, and they shall call his name Emmanuel . . ." As we showed elsewhere (Part 1, Ch. 2, art.
2), the virgin mentioned here is none other than Mary
herself, and of her the prophet says that she is a virgin
while conceiving.[273]

[269] Cf., among others, G. Herzog (pseudonym for J. Turmel), *La
Sainte Vierge dans l'histoire* (Paris, 1908), and H. Koch, *Virgo Eva —
Virgo Maria* (Berlin, 1937). A solid refutation of Koch's book may be
found in J. Lebon, in *RHE*, 34 (1938), 336–345.

[270] *DB*, 2.

[271] *DB*, 86.

[272] Many references in Roschini, *op. cit.*, 245–247.

[273] Cf. S. Bonano, above, footnote 50.

The fulfillment of this prophecy is attested to by St. Luke while describing the scene of the Annunciation: "Behold thou shalt conceive and bear a son. . . ." (Luke 1: 26–38). When Mary asks how this shall be, for she knows not man, the angel reassures her that her virginity shall remain intact: "The Holy Ghost shall come upon thee and the power of the Most High shall overshadow thee." Later on, when St. Joseph became aware of the fact that Mary was with child, he was minded to send her away quietly, but the angel appeared to him and dissipated his fears by telling him that Mary had conceived of the Holy Ghost (hence, without the aid of man), whereupon St. Joseph accepted her as his wife (Matthew 1:18–24).[274]

(3) *Tradition.* From the very beginning the Fathers and ecclesiastical writers have unanimously expressed their belief that Christ did not have a human father, and that Mary conceived Him in a miraculous and virginal manner. This is so evident that, even Harnack, a bitter foe of Mary's virginity, frankly admits that already in the second century this belief was unanimously accepted.[275] If references were needed, the following few could be given: St. Ignatius of Antioch (d. 107); Aristides (d. *c.* 140); St. Justin Martyr (d. *c.* 165); St. Irenaeus (d. 202); St. Hippolytus of Rome (d. 235);

[274] On this whole section, cf. the lengthy treatment by J. M. Vosté, O.P., *De conceptione virginali Jesu Christi* (Rome, 1933), with a scholarly refutation of non-Catholic interpretations. See also Ph. J. Donnelly, S.J., *Our Lady's Virginity "ante partum,"* in MS, 7 (1956), 13–42.

[275] A. Harnack, *Lehrbuch der Dogmengeschichte,* ed. 3, 96; ref. from Roschini *op. cit.,* 251.

Tertullian (d. 222/3); St. Clement of Alexandria (d. 211/15); Origen (d. 254/5); St. Ephraem (d. 373).[276]

D. *Objection against the Catholic Thesis.* In the first chapter of St. Matthew's gospel, the evangelist, in order to show that Christ is a descendant of David, gives the genealogy of Joseph, not of Mary. Does this not sufficiently indicate that Joseph was the natural father of Christ? The objection is strengthened by Luke 2, 33 and 48 where St. Joseph is explicitly referred to as the "father" of Our Lord. *"thy father & I have sought.*

Answer: Since St. Matthew himself elsewhere in the same gospel unequivocally teaches the virginal conception of Christ, we cannot suppose that he is here contradicting himself. Actually, the reason why he gives Joseph's genealogy is, first of all, because it is not customary in the Bible to give the genealogy of the mother; and secondly, because since St. Joseph was the true husband of Mary, he was automatically Christ's *legal* father. Therefore, in a certain sense, Christ belonged to Joseph for all civil and legal purposes. This also explains why in other passages of the New Testament (Luke 2:33, 48) Joseph is called the "father" of Christ.[277]

---

[276] St. Ignatius, *Epist. ad Smyrnaeos,* 1, 1; *PG,* 5, 708; Aristides, *Apologia,* n. 25; *PG,* 96, 1121; St. Justin, *Dialogus cum Tryphone,* 48; *PG,* 6, 580; St. Irenaeus, *Adv. haer.,* lib. 1, cap. 10, n. 1; *PG,* 7, 549; St. Hippolytus, *Contra haer. Noëti,* n. 17; *PG,* 10, 825; Tertullian, *De virginibus velandis,* n. 6; *PL,* 2, 897; St. Clement, *Stromata,* lib. 6, cap. 15; *PG,* 9, 352; Origen, *Comm. in Epist. ad Rom.,* lib. 3, n. 10; *PG,* 14, 956; St. Ephraem, *Hymni de B. Virgine,* nn. 20, 32; ed. Lamy, 2, 608; *RdJ,* 711.

[277] Cf. Vosté, *op. cit.,* 83–128; F. Ceuppens, O.P., *De Mariologia Biblica,* 2nd ed. (Turin-Rome, 1951), 68–95.

II. *Mary Was a Virgin during the Birth of Christ.*

A. *Meaning of the Thesis.* When we say that Mary was a virgin during the birth of Christ, we mean that, at the appointed time, Our Blessed Lord left the womb of His Mother in a miraculous manner, that is to say, without in any way opening the womb itself or any other part of Mary's body. In other words, as the light goes through a glass without breaking it, so Christ passed through Our Lady's body into the outside world without any detriment to her virginal seal.[278]

B. *Errors.* Mary's virginity during the birth of Our Lord (or, as it is often called, the "virgin birth" of Christ) was denied in the third century by Tertullian;[279] in the fourth century by the monk Jovinian;[280] in the sixteenth century by the Anabaptists, and later on by the Rationalists, all of whom claim that Christ came into the world like any other man.

[278] Carol (On Mary's Virginity *In Partu*), in *HPR*, 54 (February, 1954), 446–447; J. C. Fenton, *Our Lady's Virginity In Partu*, in *AER*, 130 (January, 1954), 46–53. On this point cf. the thought-provoking article by Dr. Ignacy Różycki, *De Beatae Mariae virginitate in partu*, in *CTh*, 25 (1954), 439–467. We regret to have to disagree with the author's contention that: 1) Mary's physical virginity *in partu* is not a dogma of faith, but only a theological conclusion (pp. 451 and 465); 2) Mary was not free from the pains of childbirth, except those caused by the perforation of the hymen (pp. 457–460); and 3) the text of Isaias 7:14 has nothing to do with the virginal birth of Christ. Another author who has recently questioned the validity of the traditional Catholic explanation of the virginity *in partu* is Dr. Albert Mitterer in his book *Dogma und Biologie der Heiligen Familie* (Vienna, 1952). Cf. G. Owens, C.SS.R., *Our Lady's Virginity in the Birth of Jesus*, in *MS*, 7 (1956), 45–47; also Ph. Donnelly, S.J., *Mary's Perpetual Virginity*, in *Mariology* (Carol), 2, Ch. 6, *sub prelo.*

[279] Tertullian, *De carne Christi*, cap. 23; PL. 2, 790.

[280] On Jovinian, cf. Pope Siricius' letter *Optarem*, in PL, 13, 1168–1172.

C. *Proofs of the Thesis.* The Catholic teaching concerning the virgin birth may be proved by the magisterium, by Sacred Scripture and by Tradition.

(1) *The Magisterium.* As in the case of the previous thesis, so also here, the documents of the magisterium leave no room for doubt as to the official belief of the Church from the very beginning. Thus, for example, the Apostles' Creed states that Our Lord "was conceived by the Holy Ghost, *born* of the *Virgin* Mary."[281] Again, Pope St. Siricius, in his letter to Bishop Anysisus (written in 392) condemns what he calls "the Jewish perfidy which holds that He (Christ) could not be born of a *virgin.*"[282] Pope St. Leo I, in his dogmatic letter to Flavian, patriarch of Constantinople (written in 449) unequivocally states: "She (Mary) brought Him forth without the loss of virginity, even as she conceived Him without its loss."[283] Finally, Pope St. Martin I, at the Lateran Council (649) again condemned those who refused to believe in the virgin birth.[284]

(2) *Sacred Scripture.* While the account of Christ's birth, as recorded in the gospel of St. Luke (2:5ff.), does not specify whether Christ was born in a miraculous (virginal) way or not, we do have, nevertheless, a biblical passage in the Old Testament which sufficiently establishes the Catholic teaching on this point. Thus, in the already discussed prophecy of Isaias (7:14) we are told

[281] *DB,* 6.
[282] *DB,* 91. On the authenticity of this letter, cf. below, footnote 292.
[283] *RdJ,* 2182.
[284] *DB,* 256.

that "a *virgin* shall conceive *and bear a son* . . ." As mentioned elsewhere, the original Hebrew text has it: "Behold, the *virgin* conceiving and *bearing a son.*" In other words, the prophetic vision represents Our Blessed Lady as giving birth and *simultaneously* remaining a virgin.[285]

(3) *Tradition.* There are few Catholic dogmas which can claim the unanimous support of Tradition with as much right as the dogma now under discussion. The fact is that not one single Father of the Church can be quoted as bearing witness against it. It is true that Tertullian (and perhaps Origen) held false views on this point, but they are not Fathers of the Church, nor do they represent (at least in this specific case) the mind of their contemporaries. On the other hand, we find clear testimonies in favor of the virgin birth in the writings of St. Ignatius of Antioch (d. 107), St. Irenaeus (d. 202), Clement of Alexandria (d. 211/15), St. Ephraem (d. 373), St. Ambrose (d. 397), St. Jerome (d. 419/20), St. Augustine (d. 430) and hosts of others.[286]

D. *Objections against the Catholic Thesis.* We read in St. Luke's gospel (2:22ff.): "After the days of her

[285] Cf. above, Ch. 2, art. 2.

[286] St. Ignatius, *Epist. ad Smyrnaeos*, 1, 1; PG, 5, 708; St. Irenaeus, *Demonstratio apostolicae praedicationis*, cap. 54; tr. from the Armenian by J. P. Smith, in *Ancient Christian Writers*, 16 (Westminster, Md., 1952), 83; St. Clement, *Stromata*, lib. 7, cap. 16; PG, 9, 530–531; St. Ephraem, *Explanatio evangelii concordantis*, cap. 2, n. 6; CSCO, 137, 26–27 (Armenian), 145, 20 (Latin); ref. from Burghardt, *Mary in Eastern Patristic Thought*, sect. 2; St. Ambrose, *Epist.* 42, nn. 5–6; PL, 16, 1174 (ed. 1866); St. Jerome, *Epist.* 48, n. 21; PL, 22, 510; CSEL, 54, 386; St. Augustine, *Serm.* 189, n. 2; PL, 38, 1005. On this subject, cf. J. C. Plumpe, *Some Little-Known Early Witnesses to Mary's Virginitas In Partu*, in *ThS*, 9 (1948), 567–577.

purification, according to the law of Moses, were accomplished, they (Mary and Joseph) carried Him to Jerusalem to present Him to the Lord, as it is written in the law of the Lord: Every male opening the womb shall be called holy to the Lord." Now, if Mary had given birth to Christ in a miraculous and virginal manner, why should she be subject to a law which was made for ordinary women?

Answer: Since Our Lady's virginity had remained intact during the birth of her Son, she was not, strictly speaking, bound by the law of purification. However, from motives of humility and obedience, and likewise in order not to arouse suspicion or give bad example, she willingly conformed to the external ceremony of the law. The expression "days of purification" was a *legal* term indicating the appointed time when the first-born of a family was to be presented to the temple. Since Christ was actually the first-born son of Mary, He had to be taken to the temple to be consecrated to God according to the prescriptions of the existing laws.[287]

III. *Mary Remained a Virgin after the Birth of Christ.*

A. *Meaning of the Thesis.* The Catholic teaching on this point implies: (1) that Mary did not have other

[287] Cf. B. Conway, C.S.P., *The Virgin Birth* (New York, 1924), 9–25; Vosté, *op. cit.*, 30–51; C. C. Martindale, S.J., *Christ's Virgin Birth and the Gospel of the Infancy* (London, s.a.).

children besides Christ; (2) that she did not have the slightest relations with any man; (3) that she never used her marriage rights with her legitimate husband, St. Joseph. In a word, her virginity remained intact and inviolate until death.

B. *Errors.* That Mary remained a virgin after the birth of Christ was denied by Eunomius, Apollinaris and their followers, called "Antidikomarianites"; likewise by Tertullian (after he became a heretic),[288] the monk Jovinian, Bonosus, Bishop of Sardis, and especially by the infamous Helvidius in the fourth century.[289] In more recent times this Catholic dogma has been rejected by the Anabaptists and the Rationalists.[290]

C. *Proof of the Catholic Thesis.*

(1) *The Magisterium.* The Catholic thesis is implicitly contained in the many documents of the magisterium which refer to Our Lady as "the *ever-virgin* Mary." This ancient expression, already found in an early version of the Creed called the Symbol of Epiphanius (4th century), was officially inserted in the Creed by the Second Council of Constantinople (Fifth Ecumenical Council) in the year 553.[291] It is explicitly taught by Pope St. Siricius in his letter to Bishop Anysisus in the

---

[288] Tertullian, *De virginibus velandis*, cap. 6; PL, 2, 946.
[289] Cf. St. Jerome, *Adversus Helvidium de perpetua virginitate B. Mariae*, in PL, 23, 183–211.
[290] Cf. Roschini, *op. cit.*, 245.
[291] DB, 214.

year 392;[292] by Pope St. Martin I at the Lateran Council in the year 649;[293] and Pope Paul IV who in 1555 condemned the Unitarians for denying that Mary "had always retained her virginal integrity before the birth, during the birth and perpetually after the birth (of Christ)."[294]

(2) *Sacred Scripture.* Nowhere in the Bible do we find a clear reference to the fact that Mary remained a virgin after the birth of Christ. Nevertheless, the gospel of St. Luke would seem to furnish an implicit indication when it relates that Our Lady, upon receiving the angel's announcement concerning her imminent motherhood, replied with the query: "How shall this be done, for I know not man?" (Luke 1:34). These words of Our Lady have always been interpreted to mean that she had already made a vow of perpetual virginity; if so, she certainly would not violate her solemn promise after giving birth to the Son of God in a virginal manner.[295]

(3) *Tradition.* The belief in Mary's perpetual virginity (which necessarily includes her virginity after the birth of Christ) has been so deeply rooted in Catholic

[292] *DB*, 91. Recently it has been pointed out by scholars that the true author of this letter, long attributed to Pope St. Siricius, was actually St. Ambrose of Milan. Cf. E. R. Carroll, O.Carm., *Our Lady's Virginity "post partum,"* in *MS*, 7 (1956), 75–76.

[293] *DB*, 256.

[294] *DB*, 993. On liturgical testimonies concerning the perpetual virginity, cf. P. A. Resch, S.M., *Our Blessed Mother. Outlines of Mariology* (Milwaukee, Wis., 1939), 115–117.

[295] Cf. J. J. Collins, S.J., *Our Lady's Vow of Virginity* (Luke 1:34), in *CBQ*, 5 (1943), 371–380, an objective criticism of D. Haugg's book *Das erste biblische Marienwort. Eine exegetische Studie zu Lukas 1:34* (Stuttgart, 1938).

Tradition from the very beginning, that the Fathers of the Church instinctively and vigorously rose to its defense every time it was questioned by early heretics. Among the many witnesses that could be mentioned in this connection, reference to the following will suffice: Origen, St. Ephraem, St. Hilary, St. Zeno, St. John Chrysostom, St. Epiphanius, St. Ambrose, St. Jerome, St. Augustine and many others.[296]

D. *Objections against the Catholic Thesis.*

(1) The Gospels refer to Christ as being the "first-born" son of Mary (Luke 2:7; Matthew 1:25). But Christ would not be the "first-born" unless other children (or at least one) had not been born of Mary.

Answer: According to the Mosaic law the term "first-born" was applied to him whose birth had not been preceded by another, whether others followed or not. Hence, every *only*-born is necessarily a *first*-born, but not vice versa. Since, according to the law, every mother was expected to go through certain rituals after giving birth to her first child (regardless of whether others were

<hr />

[296] Origen, *Comm. in Joannem*, lib. 1, n. 4; GCS, 10, 8; id., *Hom.* 7 *in Lucam*; GCS, 35, 49; PG, 13, 1818; id., *Comm. in Matthaeum*, tom. 10, cap. 17; GCS, 40, 21–22; PG, 13, 876–877; St. Ephraem, *Expl. evang. concordantis*, cap. 2, n. 6; CSCO, 137, 26–27 (Armenian), 145, 19–20 (Latin); St. John Chrysostom, *Hom. 5 in Matthaeum*, n. 3; PG, 57, 58; St. Epiphanius, *Panarion*, haer. 78, nn. 5–24; GCS, 37, 455–475; PG, 42, 699, 706; St. Hilary, *Comm. in Matthaeum*, cap. 1, nn. 3–4; PL, 9, 921–922; St. Zeno, *Tractatus*, lib. 2, tr. 8, 2; PL, 11, 414–415; St. Ambrose, *De institutione virginis*, cap. 5, n. 35; PL, 16, 328; St. Jerome, *Adversus Helvidium*; PL, 23, 193–216 (ed. 1865); St. Augustine, *Serm.* 196, n. 1; PL, 38, 1019. Cf. Burghardt, *Mary in Western Patristic Thought*, 126–132.

to follow or not), it is understandable that the Gospels
refer to Christ as being the "first-born" in connection
with the ceremony of His presentation in the temple.
The above interpretation is further corroborated by the
discovery in 1922 of an ancient Jewish tombstone inscription to the effect that a young mother had died
while giving birth to her "first-born" son.[297] Surely in
this case the first-born was not followed by other children.

(2) In the gospel of St. Matthew (1:18) we read:
"When His Mother Mary was espoused to Joseph, *before they came together*, she was found with child, of the
Holy Ghost." Therefore, they came together (i.e., had
intercourse) afterwards. This objection is strengthened
by what we read a little further in the same gospel
(v.25): "And he (Joseph) knew her not *till* she brought
forth her first-born son." Therefore, he knew her
(through intercourse) after the birth of Christ.

Answer: The biblical expression "to come together"
probably does not mean to have intercourse, but rather
"to dwell together under the same roof." Among the
Jews the bride did not live together with her spouse until the wedding had been solemnized. Hence, the gospel
merely tells us that, at the time of the Annunciation,
Mary had not as yet taken up her residence with St.
Joseph, although she did so afterwards.

If, however, the adversaries insist that the expression
"come together" means to have sexual relations, then we

[297] Cf. J. B. Frey, S.S.Sp., *La signification du terme "prototokos"
d'après une inscription juive*, in *Bibl*, 11 (1930), 373–390.

answer: In Sacred Scripture the terms "till" and "before" are often used in order to state what has *not* taken place before or until a specific time, regardless of whether or not it took place afterwards. For example, in the second book of Kings (6:23) we read that "Michol, the daughter of Saul, had no child *till* the day of death." Does it follow that she had a child after her death? Again, in the book of Psalms (109:1) we read of Christ: "Sit thou at my right hand, *until* I make thy enemies thy footstool." Does it follow that Christ will no longer sit at the right hand of the Eternal Father after His enemies lie defeated at His feet? Finally, if we say: "Joseph Stalin died before he made his peace with the Catholic Church," does it follow that he made his peace after death?

(3) In the New Testament there is frequent reference to the "brethren" of the Lord. For example: In Matthew 12:46; 15:55f.; Mark 3:31; 6:3; Luke 8:20; John 2:12; 7:3; Acts 1:14; I Corinthians 9:5; Galatians 1:19. In fact, the Gospels even furnish the names of these brethren, namely: James, Joseph, Simon and Judas (Matthew 13:55; Mark 6:3). How does this harmonize with Mary's perpetual virginity?

Answer: Some of the early Fathers of the Church (for example, St. Epiphanius, St. Hilary and St. Cyril of Alexandria) claimed that the men referred to in the Gospels as Christ's "brethren" were actually sons of St. Joseph by a previous marriage.[285] This explanation, however, has been generally rejected since the time of St.

Jerome principally because of the universal belief among Christians that St. Joseph, like Our Blessed Lady, had remained a virgin throughout his life.

A more plausible solution would be that the Greek term "adelphos" (i.e., "brother") is sometimes employed in the Bible as meaning also "close relative," such as cousin or nephew. For example, Lot who was a cousin of Abraham (Genesis 12:5), is also called Abraham's "brother" (Genesis 13:8); and Jacob is referred to as the "brother" of Laban (Genesis 29:15), although we know that he was actually Laban's nephew (Genesis 29:10).[298]

As to the four men (James, Joseph, Simon and Judas) mentioned as Christ's brethren in the gospel of St. Matthew (13:55), we know for certain that two of them were sons of Mary, the wife of Cleophas (Matthew 27:56), and sister of Our Lady (John 19:25). This being so, they were not brothers of Christ in the strict sense, but rather His first cousins. This is, at any rate, one of the solutions offered by Catholic scholars.[299]

SCHOLION. *Mary's Vow of Virginity.*

In order to do justice to the unexcelled degree of Mary's purity and chastity it is not sufficient to have established her bodily or external virginity. We must attribute to her also an internal virginity, a virginity of

---

[298] Cf. Roschini, *op. cit.*, 263–264.

[299] A more detailed answer to the objection may be found in Vosté, *op. cit.*, 111–128; and O. Rodríquez, *"Qui sunt fratres mei?"* (*Matthew* 12:48), in VD, 5 (1925), 132–137.

soul. By this we mean a firm desire never to lose her integrity, a desire sealed by an absolute vow of virginity.

The magisterium of the Church has never made an official pronouncement on the question, nor does Sacred Scripture contain any clear statement to that effect. However, the generally accepted thesis among Catholic theologians (against the opinion of Calvin and his disciples) is that Our Lady did make a vow of perpetual virginity before the Annunciation.[300] In support of this belief theologians produce the query which Our Lady addressed to the angel: "How shall this be done, for I know not man?" (Luke 1:34). Mary was here presenting an obstacle to the angel's proposal. This obstacle was neither natural impotence (she had already reached puberty) nor a prohibitive precept of the law (this was non-existent). Therefore, that obstacle must have been her vow of virginity.[301]

This vow of virginity did not, of course, render her marriage fictitious or useless, as Pelagius, Wycliff and others thought. It was not fictitious because the essence of the marriage contract does not lie in the use of the material rights, but rather in the rights themselves,

[300] Two notable exceptions in recent years are: D. Haugg, *Das erste biblische Marienwort* (Stuttgart, 1938), and P. Gächter, S.J., *The Chronology from Mary's Betrothal to the Birth of Christ*, in *ThS*, 2 (1941), 146–162. Cf. N. M. Flanagan, O.S.M., *Our Lady's Vow of Virginity*, in *MS*, 7 (1956), 103–121. On the question as to whether Mary's vow was conditional or absolute, cf. Roschini, *op. cit.*, 273–274; L. M. Maestu Ojanguren, O.F.M., *De voto virginitatis B. V. Mariae, praesertim juxta doctrinam Doctoris Subtilis, Joannis Duns Scoti*, in *ASC*, 11 (Rome, 1953), 115–145.

[301] Cf. Collins, *art. cit.*, and U. Holzmeister, S. J., "*Quomodo fiet istud quoniam virum non cognosco?*," in *VD*, 19 (1939), 70–77.

mutually surrendered. It was not useless, because there were several good reasons why God wished His Son to be born of a wedded mother, such as, for example, lest Christ be looked upon as illegitimate and His Mother as guilty of a sexual crime.[302]

---

[302] On Mary's marriage to St. Joseph, and related questions, cf. F. L. Filas, S.J., *Joseph and Jesus* (Milwaukee, Wis., 1952), esp. 10–20; H. Frévin, *Le mariage de la Sainte Vierge dans l'histoire de la théologie* (MS doctoral thesis submitted to the theological faculty of Lille in 1951), 263 pp.; F. Girerd, *Le mariage de la Sainte Vierge*, in NRT, 50 (1923), 449–464; G. Fournelle, O.F.M., *Our Lady's Marriage to St. Joseph*, in MS, 7 (1956), 122–129; Holzmeister, *De nuptiis Sancti Joseph*, in VD, 25 (1947), 145–149; N. López Martínes, *Porque no conozco varón* (*Luke* 1:34), in CB, 11 (1954), 333–335; M. Flunk, S.J., *Eine archäologische-exegetische Studie über die Vermählung der hl. Jungfrau mit Joseph*, in ZfkT, 12 (1888), 656–686; Maestu Ojanguren, *art. cit.*, 137–145.

CHAPTER THREE

Our Lady's Knowledge

By "KNOWLEDGE" here we mean the correct understanding of facts, the intellectual perception of truth.
Authors generally distinguish three types of knowledge:
beatific, infused, and acquired.

Preliminary Notions.

I. *Beatific* knowledge is the direct perception of God
as He is in Himself, such as the blessed have in heaven.

II. *Infused* knowledge is that which the intellect re-
ceives through a direct action on the part of God. It is
called infused *per se* if it cannot be acquired in any other
way; infused *per accidens* if it can be acquired by the
effort of the human mind, although *de facto* it is directly
communicated by God. The former does not necessarily
depend on our sensitive faculties for its use; the latter
does.[303]

III. *Acquired* knowledge is that which a person obtains by abstracting intelligible species from phan-
tasms.[304] It is called *experimental* when things previously known through infused knowledge are learned

---

[303] Cf. J. Solano, S.J., *De Verbo Incarnato*, in *Sacrae Theologiae
Summa*, (edited by the Spanish Jesuits), 3 (Madrid, 1950), 116–117.
[304] Cf. Farges-Barbedette, *Philosophia Scholastica*, 44th ed., 2 (Paris,
1928), 114–120.

through one's own experience. It is called *deductive* when it is acquired by means of a judgment or reasoning process of the intellect.

With these preliminary notions in mind, let us now review briefly the teaching of theologians concerning Our Lady's knowledge.

A. As to *beatific* knowledge, it is certain that Our Lady did not have it permanently during the course of her earthly life, for this type of cognition is proper to the blessed in heaven, while Our Lady was a wayfarer. Besides, the direct perception of the divine nature is incompatible with the virtue of faith, which Mary surely possessed in a very high degree. However, not a few theologians believe that Our Lady was granted this privilege transiently on certain eventful occasions of her life. Their reasoning is that Mary, being the Mother of God, should not be denied a privilege which was enjoyed by Moses and St. Paul during their lifetime.[305]

B. With regard to *per se infused* knowledge, the fact that Our Lady possessed it is generally admitted. The reason is that this privilege was granted by God to St. John the Baptist while in the womb of his mother, to the angels, and even to our first parents before the fall. Since Mary's endowments by far exceed those of all other creatures, it stands to reason that she, too, should have enjoyed a similar prerogative, which was in no way incongruous with her condition, but rather fitting to her dignity as Mother of God.

[305] Cf. Dublanchy, *art. cit.*, 2410–2411; Keuppens, *op. cit.*, 74.

As to the precise time when this *per se* infused knowledge was given to Our Lady, theologians are not in accord. Against St. Thomas, who taught that this privilege was exclusive to Christ,[306] some hold that Our Lady had it at the time of her Immaculate Conception, although not permanently.[307] The greater number of theologians, however, are of the opinion that God granted it to her permanently from the very first moment of her existence.[308] The grounds for their theory have already been indicated in connection with Our Lady's growth in holiness.

Just what precisely Our Lady perceived through this infused knowledge is rather difficult to determine with any degree of certitude. Most likely she did not know the intimate nature of all material (even possible) things, as Christopher de Vega and a few others have claimed,[309] because this knowledge was in no way postulated by her dignity as Mother of God. Nevertheless, she must have possessed a grasp (not necessarily perfect from the beginning) of all those natural and supernatural truths which were in some manner connected with the unique role assigned to her in the economy of salvation. One of these truths, we may be sure, was the divinity of her Son, and the related soteriological mission.[310]

[306] *Summa Theologica*, III, 27, 3.

[307] For example, Card. Lépicier, *op. cit.*, 226–228; Merkelbach, *op. cit.*, 199–201.

[308] Cf. A. d'Alès, art. *Marie*, in *DAFC*, 3, 206; Keuppens, *op. cit.*, 77–78; Roschini, *op. cit.*, 188.

[309] Cf. Ch. de Vega, S.J., *Theologia Mariana*, 1 (ed. Naples, 1866), 405–412.

[310] Cf. Roschini, *op. cit.*, 190.

As to *per accidens* infused knowledge, it is generally held that Mary did not receive it, the principal reason being that, since she already had *per se* infused knowledge, nothing seems to demand an additional miracle such as would be involved in the conferring of this extra gift. However, those who refuse to admit that Our Lady had *per se* infused knowledge (for example, Cardinal Lépicier) generally grant that she received it *per accidens.*[311]

C. Concerning *acquired* knowledge, both experimental and deductive, it is unquestionable that Our Lady possessed it "since she was subject to empirical reactions, and was endowed with an operative *intellectus agens* and with an *intellectus patiens* capable of functioning normally. As to the principal sources of Mary's information . . . they were the assiduous reading of the Sacred Scriptures[312] and, of course, the frequent discourses with her divine Son. Regarding the perfection and extent of Mary's acquired knowledge, we surmise that they must have been exceedingly great, considering that she possessed the gift of integrity and that, therefore, her intelligence retained all its native brilliance. However, as in the case of her infused knowledge, this acquired understanding must not be conceived as extending to human affairs not connected with her office

[311] Cf. Lépicier, *op. cit.,* 226. Ch. de Vega, *op. cit.,* 1, 445–450, believes that Our Lady knew, through *per accidens* infused knowledge, all the intricate problems of the natural sciences.

[312] That Our Lady was very familiar with Sacred Scripture is revealed in every verse of her canticle *Magnificat.* Cf. T. Gallus, Ad *"principium materiale"* Redemptionis objectivae, in DTPl, 57 (1954), 246–247.

as Mother of God and cooperator with her Son in the work of Redemption."[313]

SCHOLION. *Was Mary Free from Error and Ignorance?*

Closely related to the above is the question concerning Our Lady's immunity from error and from ignorance. Error implies a false judgment based on deceptive information. In the present order of things, error is a sequel of original sin which disturbed the perfect balance of our faculties. Hence, it must be excluded from Our Blessed Lady. As to ignorance, we must draw a necessary distinction. *Privative* ignorance denotes the lack of knowledge a person is expected or required to have. This type of ignorance (whether culpable or not) cannot be attributed to Our Lady because it is incompatible with her sublime dignity, with her absolute immunity from the sequels of sin, and with her gift of integrity. *Negative* ignorance, on the contrary, refers to the lack of knowledge a person is not expected or required to have. This second type of ignorance (which does not connote any moral imperfection whatever) may and should be admitted in Our Lady. The Gospels themselves support this attribution. For example, at the time of the Annunciation Our Lady asked the angel: "How shall this be done . . . ?" (Luke 1:34). While she knew that she was to be the Mother of God, obviously she was not

[313] Thus, F. J. Connell, C.SS.R., *Our Lady's Knowledge*, in *Mariology* (Carol), 2, Ch. 8.

aware of all the circumstances surrounding this fact; for example, she did not know just how her virginity would remain intact notwithstanding her motherhood of the Messias. Again, when Our Lord encountered her and St. Joseph in the temple, after the three days' loss, He said to them: " 'How is it that you sought me? Did you not know that I must be about my Father's business?' And they understood not the word that He spoke unto them." (Luke 1:49–50.) The passage does not imply that Mary was unaware that Christ was the Son of God (as some writers would have us believe), but simply that she was ignorant of the particular details relative to the specific manner in which He would fulfill His messianic mission.[314]

---

[314] On the question of Our Lady's so-called ignorance relative to the divinity of her Son, cf. E. F. Sutcliffe, S.J., *Our Lady and the Divinity of Christ*, in *Mth*, 180 (1944), 347–350. The article gave rise to an immediate counterattack from various quarters. See the pertinent literature listed in chronological order by Father E. May, O.F.M.Cap., in *MS*, 3 (1952), 122–123, footnote 18.

Prerogatives Conferred on Mary at the End of Her Life

The prerogatives conferred on Our Blessed Lady at the close of her earthly career were four: 1) immunity from corruption; 2) an anticipated resurrection; 3) her bodily Assumption; and 4) her glorification in heaven.

Of these, the anticipated resurrection has been questioned or denied by those who question or deny the fact of Mary's death, which it necessarily presupposes. We shall devote the first chapter of this section to this latter point. The other three prerogatives mentioned have already been defined by the magisterium, and are rightly considered as integral elements of one and the same truth. Hence in our second chapter we shall treat them as one prerogative under the common name of "Assumption."

Our Lady's Death

CATHOLICS have, from time immemorial, universally believed that Our Lady underwent a natural death at the close of her earthly career. Their views have differed widely as to the causes of her death, and also as to the circumstances of its time and place; but the fact itself was unquestionably accepted. This traditional thesis may be considered, therefore, as at least *theologically certain*. Some go further and declare it "proximately definable"[315] and even an article of "divine and Catholic faith."[316] Let us review briefly: 1) the adversaries of the traditional teaching; and 2) the various arguments in its favor.

I. *Adversaries*. The adversaries of the death-thesis are not all equally sure of their own position. Some merely doubt it, others openly reject it. Already in the 4th century, St. Epiphanius (d. 403) frankly confessed his ignorance concerning the final lot of Our Lady.[317] In the 6th century, or shortly after, Timothy of Jerusalem refers

[315] Thus Aldama, *op. cit.*, 398; L. Di Fonzo, O.F.M.Conv., *De Immaculatae Deiparae Assumptione post praecipua recentiora studia critica disquisitio*, in MF, 47 (1947), 71.

[316] For example, C. Koser, O.F.M., in *Calificación teológica de la Asunción*, in SM, 5 (Buenos Aires, 1950), 338.

[317] St. Epiphanius, *Panarion*, haer. 78, n. 11; PG, 42, 715–716; cf. 737.

to her as being "immortal up to now."[318] In the 18th century an anonymous Jesuit author (identified by some as Ignatius Camargo) wrote a lengthy treatise in defense of Mary's immortality.[319] In more recent times, particularly since the definition of the Immaculate Conception, the doctrine has been roundly rejected by such authors as Arnaldi, Gallus, and Roschini.[320] Others have adopted a more cautious attitude by merely questioning the validity of the arguments supporting the so-called traditional thesis. To this group belong Friethoff, Philips, and especially Jugie, who has accumulated many reasons pointing to Mary's immortality.[321]

II. *Proof of the Thesis.* The arguments in favor of the thesis that Our Lady actually died may be grouped under these headings: a) the magisterium; b) the liturgy; c) Sacred Scripture; d) tradition; and e) theological reason.

[318] Timothy of Jerusalem, *Hom. in Simeonem et Annam*; PG, 86, 246. On this author, cf. B. Capelle, O.S.B., *Les homélies liturgiques du prétendu Timothée de Jérusalem*, in EL, 63 (1949), 5–26.

[319] Cf. *Tractatus de immortalitate Beatae Virginis Mariae*, ed. C. Balić, O.F.M. (Rome, 1948). M. Ramírez, S.J., in ATG, 13 (1950), 285, does not believe that the author of this book was Camargo, as claimed by Roschini, *La Madonna secondo la fede e la teologia*, 3 (Rome, 1953), 273.

[320] D. Arnaldi, *Super definibilitate dogmatica Assumptionis corporeae B. V. M. Deiparae Immaculatae* (Turin, 1884), 32; T. Gallus, S.J., *La Vergine Immortale* (Rome, 1949); Roschini, *op. cit.*, 3, 255–295. Further references in Roschini, 273–276.

[321] C. Friethoff, O.P., *De doctrina Assumptionis corporalis B. M. V. rationibus theologicis illustrata*, in Ang, 16 (1938), 12; G. Philips, *Autour de la définibilité d'un dogme*, in Mm, 10 (1948), esp. 105–109; M. Jugie, A.A., *La mort et l'Assomption de la Sainte Vierge* (Vatican City, 1944), 539. It should be noted that C. Van Crombrugghe, who is sometimes mentioned as belonging to this group, clearly states that the fact of Mary's death must be held as *certain*. Cf. *Tractatus de Beata Virgine Maria* (Ghent, 1913), 177.

A. *The Magisterium.* To the best of our knowledge, there are no official papal documents available either in favor or against the belief that Our Lady died. There is, however, a sermon written by Pope Clement V (d. 1314) in which we read: "It must be held firmly she (Mary) really and truly rose again."[322] Obviously, the Pope presupposes that she died before rising again. In 1933 Pope Pius XI declared that the grace Our Lady received at the time of her conception was "a grace of Redemption which did not confer on her a true and proper immortality."[323] As to the teaching of Pius XII, note the controversy mentioned in the scholion at the end of this chapter.

Objection. According to a decision of the Second Council of Orange (in 529), if anyone shall say that "(corporal) death alone, which is the punishment of sin, and not sin itself . . . was transmitted through one man to the entire human race, he attributes an injustice to God."[324] Therefore, since Mary was free from Adam's sin, she should be free also from the necessity of dying.[325]

Answer. The words of the Council may be understood to mean that we would attribute an injustice to God if we supposed that He inflicted death *as a punishment* on an individual who had never contracted sin. It does not mean

---

[322] Clement V, *Sermo Assumptionis;* cod. vat. lat. 916, fol. 246rb; quoted by Balić, *Testimonia de Assumptione B. V. Mariae ex omnibus saeculis,* pars prior (Rome, 1948), 349.

[323] Pius XI, in *OssR,* August 16–17, 1933.

[324] *DB,* 175.

[325] Thus Roschini, *op. cit.,* 3, 234–235.

that God would be unjust if He allowed an innocent person to die *for some other reason extrinsic to sin.*[326]

B. *The Liturgy.* It is well known that the liturgy of the Church, which reflects the mind of the magisterium in doctrinal matters, contains repeated allusions to the specific manner in which Our Lady departed this life. In fact, one of the very earliest liturgical feasts in honor of Mary had for its object to commemorate her death. The data concerning the origins of this observance—a subject so widely discussed in recent times—may be summarized as follows:

The feast of Mary's death (in Greek: *koimesis,* i.e., "falling asleep") was first celebrated in Alexandria (Egypt) in the first half of the 6th century on January 16. Some forty years after its introduction, Emperor Maurice (588–602) decreed that the observance be transferred to August 15 throughout the Byzantine Empire.[327]

In the first half of the 7th century, St. John, Bishop of Thessalonica (610–649) established the feast in his diocese, and from there it passed on to Rome under the pontificate of Theodore I (642–649).[328]

In the second half of this same century, the famous collect *Veneranda* was composed on the initiative of Pope Sergius I (687–701) to be recited at the beginning

[326] Cf. Carol, *The Immaculate Conception and Mary's Death,* in OLD, 9, Feb. (1955), 308; also Balić, *A propósito de la reciente controversia sobre la definibilidad de la Asunción de la Bienaventurada Virgen,* in SM, 5 (Buenos Aires, 1950), 363–374.

[327] Cf. P. Gassó, O.S.B., *La Asunción en la liturgia. Sobre los orígenes de la fiesta,* in EM, 6 (1947), 138–139.

[328] Cf. Gassó, *art. cit.,* 145–146.

of a procession held in connection with the feast. The
collect reads: "O Lord, worthy indeed of veneration is
the feast of this day on which the holy Mother of God
underwent temporal death, but could not be overcome
by the bonds of death . . ."[329] It is significant that this
oration formed part of the Roman liturgy until the 13th
century, and is still used in the Gallican and Milanese
rites, and also in the missals of the Cistercians, Premon-
stratensians and Dominicans.[330] Likewise, the prayer
Subveniat, in which Mary's death is attributed to the
"condition of (her) flesh," was part of the Mass of the
Assumption for many centuries until 1950 when the new
text of the Mass was composed.

Objection. In 1950 the oration *Subveniat* was elim-
inated from the Roman liturgy and another was sub-
stituted which makes no reference to Mary's death. This
change, purposely introduced, automatically neutralizes
all previous references to the contrary.[331]

Answer. The substitution alluded to indicates that, at
the present time, the Church simply wishes to refrain
from openly and officially taking sides in the current controversy. The new prayer says nothing either in favor or
against Mary's death. As such, it is merely a negative
argument, and hence cannot militate against the numerous, positive liturgical texts which mirrored the mind of

[329] *Sacramentarium Gregorianum; PL,* 88, 133. On this prayer, cf.
Capelle, *Mort et Assomption de la Vierge dans l'oraison "Veneranda,"*
in *EL,* 66 (1952), 241–251.

[330] Cf. Capelle, *L'Assunzione e la liturgia* (Rome, 1953), 35.

[331] Cf. Gallus, *Ad questionem mortis post bullam "Munificentissimus
Deus,"* in *Mm,* 15 (1953), 124; Roschini, *op. cit.,* 3, 290.

the Church for so many centuries. As a matter of fact, the fifth lesson of the new office for the same feast still retains a passage from St. John Damascene in which Our Lady's death is expressly affirmed.

C. *Sacred Scripture*. The Bible makes no explicit mention of Mary's final lot. Perhaps the Protoevangelium (Genesis 3:15) may be said to contain a veiled reference to her death. As we have seen elsewhere[332] the solemn words which God addressed to the serpent in the garden of Eden foretold Our Lady's intimate share in the redemptive mission of her Son. Since this mission, in the present economy, calls for the death of the Redeemer as a means of destroying the power of Satan, we might conclude that the Redeemer's partner should likewise die in order to achieve a greater conformity with Him in His triumph. This line of reasoning appeals to not a few modern theologians[333] although it is vigorously rejected by others.[334]

Objection. It is clear from Sacred Scripture (e.g., Genesis 2:17 and Romans 5:12) that, in the present order of things, death is the penal consequence of original sin personally contracted. Since Our Lady was completely preserved from the latter, she should be free also from the former.[335]

[332] Cf. above, Part 1, Ch. 5, art. 1.
[333] Cf. B. Kloppenburg, O.F.M., *Questões teológicas em torno da morte da Mãe de Jesus*, in REB, 9 (1949), esp. 329–333; Bover, *La Asunción de María; estudio teológico histórico* . . . (Madrid, 1947), 78.
[334] Cf. E. A. Wuenchel, C.SS.R., *The Definability of the Assumption*, in PCTSA, 2 (1947), 98, footnote 97.
[335] Thus Roschini, *op. cit.*, 3, 276–278. Cf. also his article *The Assumption and the Immaculate Conception*, in Thom, 14 (1950), 59–71.

Answer. These and similar passages of Sacred Scripture may well be interpreted in the sense that death (besides being natural to man) is also a punishment *for those who contract original sin.* They say nothing about the unique case of a person not involved in Adam's prevarication.[336] St. Paul's text obviously does not apply to Our Lady. If it did, we would have to conclude rather that she, too, had contracted original sin, for he excludes no one from this universal law. Therefore, from the fact that Mary was free from original sin, only one conclusion may be drawn, namely: her death was not in punishment for sin personally contracted. It does not follow, in good logic, that she did not die for some other reason. The very fact that she had a human body, which is inherently mortal,[337] is a sufficient reason postulating her death, as the Church herself openly declared in her liturgy for so many centuries.

D. *Tradition.* It is principally on Tradition that the truth of Mary's death would seem to rest. We shall give here only an outline of the pertinent testimony.

In the 3rd century, Origen (d. 254/255) makes a passing remark to the effect that Our Lady had "re-

---

[336] E. Sauras, O.P., in *La Asunción de la Santísima Virgen* (Valencia, 1950), 129–154, endeavors to establish that Our Lady died, not because she had contracted original sin, but, among other reasons, because she incurred the debt of that sin. For those who refuse to include Our Lady under the law of sin (as we do), the author's reasoning process is devoid of all foundation. Besides, even if Our Lady had incurred the debt of sin, this fact alone would be insufficient to postulate her death. Cf. Roschini, *L'Assunzione; rassegna bibliografica di alcuni scritti recenti,* in *Mm,* 13 (1951), 307.

[337] Cf. Carol, *art. cit.,* 305–306.

mained a virgin until her death."[338] An equally casual, though clear, reference is found also in the writings of St. Ephraem (d. 373).[339] His contemporary, St. Gregory of Nyssa (d. c. 394) is likewise explicit on this point.[340] St. Augustine (d. 430) goes so far as to state (wrongly, of course) that Our Lady died "on account of Adam's sin."[341]

The apocryphal literature known as the *Transitus Mariae* ("The Passing of Mary"), which began to be disseminated in the 6th century,[342] unanimously agrees that Mary died.[343] At about the same time, James of Sarug (d. 521) even furnishes us a detailed account of Our Lady's funeral,[344] and at the end of the 7th century pseudo-Modestus of Jerusalem relates how Our Lord Himself came to raise His Mother from the tomb and to take her to the glory of heaven.[345]

[338] Origen, *Comm. in Joannem*, fragm. 31; GCS, *Origenes Werke*, ed. Preuschen (Leipzig, 1903), 4, 506. The authenticity of the fragment is disputed by some. Cf. Balić, *Testimonia . . .*, 1, 6, footnote 1.

[339] St. Ephraem, *Hymni de beata Maria*, 15, n. 2; ed. Lamy, 2 (Malines, 1886), 584.

[340] St. Gregory, *De virginitate*, cap. 13; PG, 46, 377.

[341] St. Augustine, *Enarratio in Ps.* 34, n. 3; PL, 36, 335.

[342] Cf. M. Gordillo, S.J., *La muerte de María en la iglesia de Jerusalén*, in EM, 9 (1950), 50–52; Bover, *Los apócrifos y la tradición asuncionista*, in EM, 6 (1947), 100–104.

[343] A. C. Rush, C.SS.R., *Mary in the Apocrypha*, in *Mariology* (Carol), 1, 166–170; Bover, *op. cit.*, 18–22.

[344] James of Sarug, *De transitu Dei Genitricis*, ed. Baumstark, in OC, 5 (1905), 92–98.

[345] Pseudo-Modestus of Jerusalem, *Encomium in dormitionem sanctissimae Dominae nostrae Deiparae*, n. 14; PG, 86, 3312. On those who favor, and those who doubt the authenticity of this piece, cf. Balić, *Testimonia . . .*, 1, 77, footnote 2; R. Laurentin, *Court traité de théologie mariale* (Paris, 1953), 168.

From the 8th to the 13th century, the references become more explicit and categorical. Among the more important witnesses of this period we note the following: St. Germain of Constantinople (d. 733), St. Andrew of Crete (d. 740), St. John Damascene (d. 749), St. Theodore Studite (d. 826), St. Joseph the Hymnographer (d. 883), Otto of Vercelli (d. 960), St. Peter Damian (d. 1072), Blessed Amadeus of Lausanne (d. 1159), and Richard of St. Victor (d. 1173).[346]

From the 13th to the 19th century the belief in Mary's death is unquestionably accepted by Catholic writers and theologians everywhere.[347] In more recent times, particularly after the definition of the Immaculate Conception, the champions of the immortality theory have increased in number (as indicated at the beginning of this chapter); but even now the vast majority still adheres to the traditional belief.

Objection. It is evident that, from the very beginning,

[346] St. Germain, *In S. Dei Genitricis dormitionem*, serm. 1; PG, 98, 346; St. Andrew, *Orat. 13 in dormit. S. Deiparae*; PG, 97, 1082; St. John Damascene, *Encomium in dormit. Dei Genitricis*, hom. 2, n. 2; PG, 96, 726; St. Theodore, *Laudatio in dormit. Deiparae*; PG, 99, 723; St. Joseph the Hymnographer, *Mariale. In festivitate obdormitionis b. Virginis*, can. 3, ode 5; PG, 105, 1002; Otto (or Atto) of Vercelli, *In Assumptione b. Dei Genitricis semper Virginis Mariae*, serm. 17; PL, 134, 857; St. Peter Damian, Serm. 64, *De S. Joanne Apost. et Evangelista*; PL, 144, 870–871; St. Amadeus, Homil. 7, *de B. Virginis obitu* . . . ; PL, 196, 1341–1342; Richard of St. Victor, *Expl. in Cant. Cant.*, cap. 42; PL, 196, 523–524. Cf. A. Rivera, C.M.F., *La muerte de María en la tradición hasta la Edad Media (siglos I al VIII)*, in EM, 9 (1950), 71–100.

[347] Cf. Balić, *La controversia acerca de la muerte de María Santísima desde la Edad Media hasta nuestros días*, in EM, 9 (1950), 101–123.

information concerning Mary's death was based on the authority of the apocrypha; hence it cannot be considered as representative of an authentic Catholic tradition.[348] Furthermore, this so-called tradition, if it existed, would bear on a purely historical fact not connected with any revealed truth, and therefore would not argue to a divine revelation.[349]

Answer. As we have indicated above, some of the witnesses to Mary's death actually antedate the appearance of the apocryphal literature of the *Transitus*. Besides, the very fact that the apocrypha unanimously agree on Mary's death while disagreeing on many other details surrounding the event, shows that they reflect a previous belief in this doctrine. As to the further contention that Mary's death is a *purely* historical fact, we reply that it is not so; it is likewise a *dogmatic* fact, closely connected with several other truths of revelation and doctrinal questions relative to the inherently mortal nature of the human body, the absence of the preternatural gifts in the children of Adam, and Our Lady's predestination as Christ's partner in the work of Redemption.[350]

E. *Theological Reason.* All Catholics agree that Mary's death was not due to her having contracted original sin, for this view was condemned in 1567 by

[348] Thus Roschini, *La Madonna secondo la fede e la teologia*, 3, 280. Cf. also Jugie, *La mort et l'Assomption* . . . , 103–171, esp. 170; Gallus, *La Madonna Assunta* (Rome, 1951), 68–69.

[349] Roschini, *op. cit.*, 279.

[350] Cf. B. Aperribay, O.F.M., *La muerte de la Santísima Virgen; ¿problema meramente histórico o también teológico?*, in EM, 9 (1950), 17–42.

Pope St. Pius V,[351] and goes counter to the dogma of the Immaculate Conception. But there are other reasons which, in the mind of theologians, would seem to corroborate the traditional teaching on this point.[352] We shall summarize here the most important ones:

(1) The human nature which Mary assumed was, of itself, liable to dissolution. She did not possess the privilege of immortality which was lost by Adam for all his descendants. Mary, it is true, was immune from Adam's sin, but this was due to a special privilege which did not carry with it the preternatural gifts conferred on Adam before his sin (such as impassibility and immortality). Hence, the very fact that Mary belonged to the human family postulates her death. This is the opinion of many theologians, among whom we may mention: Suárez, Merkelbach, Bonnefoy, Balić, Sauras, Boyer, Lercher, and Aldama.[353]

In harmony with our theory concerning Mary's predestination, it is more exact to say that Our Lady lacked the gift of immortality, not because she "lost" it in

[351] DB, 1073.

[352] Cf. Aldama, La muerte de María y el concepto integral del misterio asuncionista, in EM, 9 (1950), 227–238.

[353] Suárez, De mysteriis vitae Christi, disp. 21, sect. 1, nn. 1–2; opera omnia, 19 (Paris, 1860), 313; Merkelbach, op. cit., 267–270; Bonnefoy, L'Assomption de la Très-Sainte Vierge et sa prédestination, in SM, 4 (Montreal, 1948), 318–326; Balić, De definibilitate Assumptionis B. Virginis Mariae in coelum (Rome, 1945), 52–53; Sauras, Definibilidad de la Asunción de la Santísima Virgen, in EM, 6 (1947), 47–48; Ch. Boyer, Raisons de la mort de la T.-S. Vierge, in SM, 6 (Paris, 1950), 129–130; L. Lercher, Institutiones Theologiae Dogmaticae, 2nd ed., 3 (Innsbruck, 1934), 354; Aldama, op. cit., 401. Further references may be found in B. Kloppenburg, De relatione inter peccatum et mortem (Rome, 1951), 171–173.

Adam, but rather because God had decreed that she
would have a human body (which is intrinsically mortal,
regardless of sin) so that she might share the lot of her
Son as Redeemer.

(2) According to others, the above reason is not
satisfactory because it seems to make Mary suffer the
consequences of a sin in which she had no part. For this
second group, Our Lady enjoyed the privilege of immortality *de jure* (due to her Immaculate Conception),
although *de facto* she died in order to fulfill the special
mission entrusted to her by God. In other words, Mary
was immortal *by right*, but she freely renounced that
right so as to be able to discharge her office as Coredemptrix of the human race. Among the chief exponents of
this opinion are: Cardinal Lépicier, Janssens, Bover,
Koser, Kloppenburg, O'Connell, and Crisóstomo de
Pamplona.[354]

But regardless of whether or not Mary had a *right* to
immortality, the principal theological reason postulating
her death seems to be her role as Coredemptrix. Our
Blessed Lord took unto Himself a human body like ours,
subject to passibility and death, in order that by His

[354] Lépicier, *op. cit.*, 356–361; Janssens, *op. cit.*, 864; Bover, *op. cit.*,
11–12 and 255–258; Koser, *A definibilidade da Assunção de Nossa Sen-
hora*, in REB, 7 (1947), 270; Kloppenburg, *op. cit.*, 182–188; R. V.
O'Connell, S.J., *Mary's Assumption* (New York, 1930), 16–17; *Crisóstomo de Pamplona*, O.F.M.Cap., *De la Inmaculada a la Asunción*, in
EstF, 55 (1954), 99–170; this author had previously held the opposite
view in his article *La muerte de la Santísima Virgen a la luz de la Sagrada
Escritura, de la Tradición y de la teología*, in SM, 3 (Madrid, 1948),
157; C. Feckes, *Das Mysterium der göttlichen Mutterschaft* (Paderborn,
1937), 115; J. Linden, S.J., *Die leibliche Aufnahme Mariä in den Himmel*, in ZfkT, 30 (1906), 205–207.

death He might destroy the empire of sin and death. Since Our Blessed Lady was associated with the Savior, by an indissoluble bond, throughout this redemptive process, it seems natural that she, too, should offer the supreme sacrifice of her life to the same end and to obtain the same effects, although on a different plane.

SCHOLION. The Question of Mary's Death after the Munificentissimus Deus.

On November 1, 1950, Pope Pius XII, gloriously reigning, issued the bull *Munificentissimus Deus* solemnly defining Our Blessed Lady's Assumption into heaven. As it was to be expected, theologians everywhere immediately set out to submit every word of the new document to a careful scrutiny, each one endeavoring to discover in it at least an indirect confirmation of his personal views concerning Mary's death. The various opinions expressed at the end of their minute analysis may be summarized as follows:

With but one or two exceptions,[355] *all* theologians frankly admit that in *Munificentissimus Deus* Pius XII

---

[355] For example, B. García Rodríquez, C.M.F., *La razón teológica en la Constitución "Munificentissimus Deus,"* in *EphM*, 1 (1951), 48–49; id., *Una polémica sobre la muerte de María*, ibid., 3 (1953), 55–72; L. M. Simon, O.M.I., *La Bulle "Munificentissimus Deus" et la mort de la Très-Sainte Vierge*, in *Mm*, 14 (1952), 339. These two theologians believe that Our Lady's death was *implicitly defined* by Pius XII. On the other hand, A. López Quintas, O. de M., in his article *Sugerencias sobre la definición dogmática de la Asunción* (*Est*, 7 [1951], 215–232) defends the incredible thesis that it was rather Mary's immortality that was defined by the Pope.

purposely refrained from *defining* the thesis of Mary's death. Nevertheless, their views differ as to the present status of the death-thesis:

I. Some few (for example, Roschini, Gallus, Jugie, Rossi) believe that the theory of Mary's death has lost most (if not all) of its force in the light of the new papal document.[356] Their reasons:

A. The Pope not only did not define Mary's death (as many had expected and desired), but whenever he mentions it in the bull, he is referring to someone else's views, not to his own.

B. In the bull the Pope stresses the fact that, since Mary was conceived without original sin, she was not subject to the law of corruption.[357]

C. In the new Mass for the Assumption (issued simultaneously with the bull) the Pope substitutes for the old oration *Subveniat* a new one which makes no mention whatever of Mary's death.

II. Others (Bonnefoy, Cuervo, F. de P. Solá, etc.) feel that the thesis of Mary's death has been clearly endorsed (though not defined) in the new bull.[358] Reasons:

[356] Roschini, *La Madonna* . . . , 3, 261–262; Gallus, *Quaestio mortis B. V. Mariae post bullam "Munificentissimus Deus,"* in DTPl, 55 (1952), 3–15; M. A. Rossi, O. de M., *La Bula dogmática "Munificentissimus Deus" y la muerte de la Santísima Virgen María,* in Est, 7 (1951), 394, n. 2; Jugie, *La définition du dogma de l'Assomption,* in ATh, 11 (1951), 104–105; J. Loncke, *De dogmatica definitione Assumptionis Mariae corporeae,* in CBrg, 47 (1951), 347.
[357] Cf. *Munificentissimus Deus,* ed. The Paulist Press, New York, (1951), p. 20, paragr. 40; cf. also p. 6, nn. 4–5; AAS, 42 (1950), 754.
[358] Bonnefoy, *La bulle dogmatique "Munificentissimus Deus"* (1 nov. 1950), in EphM, 1 (1951), 105–108; M. Cuervo, O.P., *Reflexiones* [sobre la bula Munificentissimus Deus], in CT, 78 (1951), 22–23;

A. In one paragraph of the document the Pope states that the faithful, under the guidance of their legitimate shepherds (the bishops), did not hesitate to admit that Our Lady had actually died.[359]

B. Most of the witnesses enumerated by the Pope in favor of the Assumption mention also Mary's death. Hence, the Pope, implicitly at least, endorses their views.[360]

III. Others, finally (Balic, Filograssi, etc.) claim that the Holy Father purposely left the question of Mary's death in the same status as before. For this group, the bull neither endorses nor rejects the thesis that Our Lady died.[361]

Conclusion:

Having carefully examined the reasons pro and con, we sincerely believe that, while the first two opinions are supported by valid arguments, the third is more objective and realistic.

Francisco de Paula Solá, S.J., *La muerte de la Santísima Virgen en la Constitución Apostólica "Munificentissimus Deus,"* in EM, 12 (1952), 156.

[359] Cf. *Munificientissimus Deus,* ed. The Paulist Press (New York, 1951), p. 9, n. 14; AAS, 42 (1950), 757.

[360] See a brief analysis of these testimonies in F. de P. Solá, *art. cit.,* 138–147; also, but from the opposite view, Gallus, *Ad questionem mortis post bullam "Munificentissimus Deus,"* in Mm, 15 (1953), 123–139.

[361] Balić, *De Constitutione Apostolica "Munificentissimus Deus" disquisitio dogmatico-apologetica* (Rome, 1951), 6; J. Filograssi, S.J., *Constitutio Apostolica "Munificentissimus Deus"* (1 novembris, 1950), in Gr, 31 (1950), 517–518.

CHAPTER TWO

Our Lady's Glorious Assumption

AFTER Our Lady died, her sacred body remained miraculously incorrupt in the tomb until the time when, reunited with her soul, it was taken to the glory of heaven where she enjoys the beatific vision and reigns with her divine Son as Queen of the universe. In treating this final Marian prerogative, we shall consider briefly the following points: I) the Catholic Dogma; II) errors in this connection; and III) proofs of the Dogma as embodied in the papal bull *Munificentissimus Deus.*

I. *The Catholic Dogma:* "The Immaculate Mother of God, the ever Virgin Mary, having completed the course of her earthly life, was assumed body and soul into heavenly glory." This thesis is *de fide,* i.e., an article of our holy faith, defined as such by Pope Pius XII on November 1, 1950 in the Apostolic Constitution *Munificentissimus Deus.*[362]

As explained in the preceding chapter, the traditional belief among Catholics has been that Mary's Assumption was preceded by her death and resurrection. For this reason, many theologians were of the opinion (shared by a few even now)[363] that Mary's death and resurrection were *essential* elements of her Assumption, at least in the concrete order. In the light of the papal

---

[362] AAS, 42 (1950), 770; Paulist Press edition, p. 22, paragr. 44.
[363] Solá, *art. cit.,* 155.

pronouncement quoted above, this view is no longer tenable. However, it is still permissible to hold that Mary's death and resurrection constitute integral elements of the prerogative defined, if the latter be considered in its fuller and broader concept. The point to be emphasized here is that Mary's Assumption has been defined by the Church; her death and resurrection have not.

II. *Errors:* In the 7th century, Adamnanus (d. 704), abbot of a monastery on the island of Iona (near Scotland), expressed his doubts on the subject of the Assumption when he wrote: "No one knows for certain where she (Mary) awaits her resurrection."[364] About the same time, the celebrated English theologian, Venerable Bede (d. 735), substantially reproduces the uncertainty of Adamnanus.[365] In the Middle Ages, owing particularly to the influence of the famous *Epistola ad Paulam et Eustochium,*[366] falsely attributed to St. Jerome, but actually written by the monk Paschasius Radbertus (d. 860),[367] many Catholic writers showed undue reserve and even doubt concerning the Assumption[368] Finally, from the 16th century on, and particularly after the solemn definition of Pius XII, Protestants have vigor-

---

[364] Adamnanus, *De locis sanctis,* lib. 1, cap. 12; CSEL, 39, 240.
[365] St. Bede, *Liber de locis sanctis,* cap. 5; CSEL, 39, 309.
[366] Pseudo-Jerome, *Epist. ad Paulam et Eustochium;* PL, 30, 122–142.
[367] As has been established beyond doubt by A. Agius, O.S.B., in *JTS,* 24 (1923), 176; C. Lambot, O.S.B., in *RB,* 46 (1934), 271; H. Barré, in *BSFEM,* 7 (1949), 70–73.
[368] Cf. S. Alameda, O.S.B., *La desorientación asuncionista de los siglos VIII-XIII y sus causas,* in *EM,* 6 (1947), 203–221; Balić, *Testimonia* . . . , 1, 184–194.

ously opposed the Catholic teaching on this point, on the pretext that it is not warranted by revelation.[369]

III. *Proofs of the Dogma:* Since the glorified state of Mary's body and soul in heaven is a fact which does not fall within the province of our senses, it stands to reason that eye-witnesses cannot possibly vouch for it: it simply cannot be established by means of historical or documentary evidence. Hence, the only way we can arrive at the knowledge of this Marian prerogative is by a revelation on the part of Almighty God. This revelation may be explicit or implicit, formal or virtual. Although most theologians would seem to favor a formally implicit revelation in the case of Mary's Assumption, the bull of the definition simply states that the doctrine was "revealed by God," without any further specification. How did Pius XII arrive at the conclusion that the Assumption was "revealed by God?" By the evidence which emerges from the following sources, which he enumerates in the Apostolic Constitution: A) the unanimous consensus of the Church teaching (or magisterium); B) Sacred Scripture; C) Sacred Tradition; D) the Sacred Liturgy; and E) the connection between the Assumption and other Catholic truths. Let us now summarize each of these arguments.

---

[369] Cf. S. Bonano, C.M.F., *Protestant Reaction to the Definition of the Assumption,* in *EphM,* 1 (1951), 282–284; A. Bea, S.J., *La definizione dell'Assunta e i protestanti,* in *SM,* 8 (Rome, 1954), 75–92; F. Cavalli, S.J., *Echi del dogma dell'Assunzione tra i protestanti,* in *CC,* 102 (1951), 31–46.

A. *Unanimous Consent of the Magisterium.* On May 1, 1946, Pope Pius XII addressed his encyclical letter *Deiparae Virginis* to all the bishops of the Catholic world asking them these two questions: 1) whether they believed that the Assumption could be defined as a dogma of our faith; 2) whether they, and the flock committed to their care, desired the proposed definition. The papal letter was answered by 1232 residential bishops (i.e., 98% of the total). Of these, 1210 (i.e., 98.2%) answered in the affirmative; 16 bishops hesitated concerning the opportuneness of the definition; only 6 doubted that the Assumption could be defined[370] Such amazing unanimity has seldom been recorded in the annals of the Church. Now, since the vast majority of bishops in union with the Holy See cannot possibly err in doctrinal matters, the Holy Father rightly inferred that the Assumption *was* a revealed truth. Judging from the general tenor of the papal document, one gathers that this is considered by the Pope the most cogent argument in justification of the dogmatic definition.[371]

B. *Sacred Scripture.* Before the papal pronouncement of Nov. 1, 1950, not a few scholars held the opinion

[370] Cf. statistics in G. Hentrich, S.J., *De motu assumptionistico hodierno*, in *ASC*, 10 (Rome, 1953), 5. The innumerable petitions addressed by the bishops and others to the Holy See have been collected by G. Hentrich and R. de Moos, S.J., in their monumental work *Petitiones de Assumptione corporea B. V. Mariae in coelum definienda ad Sanctam Sedem delatae . . .* , 2 vols. (Rome, 1942).

[371] Cf. *Munificentissimus Deus*, Paulist Press edition, p. 8, n. 12.

that the Bible was silent on the subject of Mary's Assumption.[372] After the bull *Munificentissimus Deus* this view is no longer tenable, for the Pope unequivocally states that all the arguments of the Fathers and theologians in favor of the Marian prerogative are based, ultimately, on Sacred Scripture.[373] The Bible, of course, nowhere makes an *explicit* mention concerning Our Lady's Assumption, but this doctrine is undoubtedly implied in the Protoevangelium (Genesis 3:15). It is on this biblical passage that Pius XII places particular emphasis, arguing substantially in this manner: In Genesis 3:15 Our Blessed Lady is foreshadowed as intimately sharing the identical, absolute victory of her Son over Satan. Now, according to the Apostle St. Paul (Romans 5-8; 1 Corinthians 15, 24, 26, 54, 57; Hebrews 2: 14-15), the consequences of Satan's seduction are sin and death. Therefore, in imitation of her Son, Mary, too, triumphed over sin (through her Immaculate Conception), and over death (through her glorious Assumption).[374] This is considered by many theologians the most important biblical argument in favor of Mary's prerogative, and it was, in fact, frequently exploited by the bishops in their petitions to the Holy See.[375]

[372] Thus B. Altaner, *Zur Frage der Definibilität der Assumptio B.M.V.*, in *ThR*, 45 (1949), 131 ff.

[373] Cf. Bea, *La Sacra Scrittura "ultimo fondamento" del dogma dell'Assunzione*, in *CC*, 101 (1950), 354-360.

[374] AAS, 42 (1950), 768-769. English edition, p. 20, n. 39.

[375] Cf. Carol, *The Apostolic Constitution "Munificentissimus Deus" and Our Blessed Lady's Coredemption*, in AER, 125 (October, 1951), 255-273; Hentrich-de Moos, *op. cit.*, 2, 732-734, mention some 311 prelates who invoke the Protoevangelium as a basis for the Assumption.

C. *Sacred Tradition*. In spite of serious investigation, scholars have been unable to discover any historical record pointing to belief in the Assumption during the first three centuries of Christianity.[376] The oldest extant witnesses happen to be the apocryphal writings known as the *Transitus Mariae* which date back probably to the middle of the 6th century. One of the most important of these was the one widely diffused under the assumed authorship of St. Melito, Bishop of Sardes.[377] While these apocryphal writings are admittedly spurious and contain a good deal of fiction—some of it fantastic and contradictory—nevertheless, with moral unanimity, they will agree on the specific point of Mary's Assumption, and hence may be considered as an expression of the prevalent belief among contemporary Christians.[378]

In the 6th century we have, in the West, the categorical statement of St. Gregory of Tours (d. 593), who writes: "The Lord commanded the holy body (of Mary after her death) to be borne on a cloud to Paradise where, reunited to its soul and exulting with the elect, it enjoys the everlasting bliss of eternity."[379] In

[376] Cf. O. Faller, S.J., *De priorum saeculorum silentio circa Assumptionem B. Mariae Virginis* (Rome, 1946); C. F. De Vine, C.SS.R., *The Fathers of the Church and the Assumption*, in SM, 4 (Montreal, 1947), 399–410; J. Duhr, S.J., *The Glorious Assumption of the Mother of God* (New York, 1950), 15–40.

[377] Pseudo-Melito, *Transitus Mariae*; PG, 5, 1231–1240; critical ed. by C. Tischendorf, *Apocalypses apocryphae . . .* (Leipzig, 1866), 124–136; cf. Balić, *Testimonia . . .*, 1, 137–147.

[378] Cf. A. Rush, *Mary in the Apocrypha*, in *Mariology* (Carol), 1, 170–175; id., *The Assumption in the Apocrypha*, in AER, 116 (1947), 5–31.

[379] St. Gregory of Tours, *Libri miraculorum*, lib. 1: *De gloria beatorum martyrum*, cap. 4; PL, 71, 708.

the East, Theodosius, patriarch of Alexandria (d. 567), bears witness to the same belief.[380]

From the 7th century on, Our Lady's Assumption is frequently proclaimed by the Fathers and ecclesiastical writers. Thus, in the East, we have the explicit testimony of pseudo-Modestus of Jerusalem, St. Germain of Constantinople (d. 733), St. Andrew of Crete (d. 740), St. John Damascene (d. 749) and St. Joseph the Hymnographer (d. 883).[381] In the West, pseudo-Augustine (Ratramnus?), belonging to the 9th century,[382] St. Fulbert of Chartres (d. 1029), St. Amadeus of Lausanne (d. 1159) and many others.[383] There are, it is true, some

[380] Theodosius of Alexandria, *The Falling Asleep of Mary*, English ed. by F. Robinson in *Coptic Apocryphal Gospels* (Cambridge, 1896), *Texts and Studies*, 4(2), 125; ref. from Balić, *Testimonia . . .* , 1, 48.

[381] Pseudo-Modestus, *Encomium in dormit. Deiparae*, n. 14; *PG*. 86, 3311 (cf. above, footnote 345); St. Germain, *In S. Dei Genitricis dormit.*, serm. 3; *PG*, 98, 370; St. Andrew, *In dormit. SS. Deiparae*, orat. 13; *PG*, 97, 1079–1082; St. John Damascene, *Encomium in dormit. Dei Genitricis*, hom. 1, n. 12; *PG*, 96, 719; St. Joseph the Hymnographer, *Mariale. In festivitate obdormit. B. Virginis*, can. 3, ode 5; *PG*, 105, 1002.

[382] Pseudo-Augustine (Ratramnus of Corbie), *De Assumptione B. Virginis Mariae*, cap. 5–8; *PL*, 40, 1145–1148. This is not to be confused with the other Pseudo-Augustine, *In festo Assumptionis B. Mariae sermo*, most likely written by Ambrose Autpertus (d. c. 780), and preserved in *PL*, 39, 2129–2134. This latter sermon, unlike the former, shows considerable reserve and even doubt on the question of Mary's bodily Assumption. On the former work, cf. G. Quadrio, S.D.B., *Il trattato "De Assumptione Beatae Mariae Virginis" dello pseudo-Agostino e il suo influsso nella teologia assunzionistica latina* (Rome, 1951). Incidentally, Quadrio attributes the famous sermon, not to Ratramnus of Corbie, but to Alcuin (p. 409).

[383] St. Fulbert, *De nativit. Mariae Virginis*, serm. 5; *PL*, 141, 325; St. Amadeus, *De B. Virginis obitu . . .* , homil. 7; *PL*, 196, 1341–1342. Many more testimonies of this period may be found in I. Ruidor, S.J., *La Asunción corporal de María a los cielos en los escritores eclesiásticos de la primera mitad del siglo XII*, in *EE*, 25 (1951), 343–360.

writers of this period who express doubts in this matter, as we saw above, under the heading of "errors."[384]

From the 13th century on, up to the present time, the moral unanimity of Catholic theologians, both in the East and in the West, unhesitatingly teach the doctrine of Mary's Assumption.[385] The argument from Tradition, as outlined above, clearly shows that it would be impossible to prove Our Lady's Assumption by means of a purely historical method. We simply do not have an uninterrupted chain of testimonies linking the desired extremes; and particularly the wide gap between the apostolic age and the 5th and 6th century remains unbridged. However, as we pointed out before, the Assumption defined by Pius XII is not a historical but rather a dogmatic fact; hence it must be established by means of a dogmatic, not historical, method. In other words, we are dealing here with the contents of divine revelation, not with historical data.

The argument from Tradition, then, derives its force from the following consideration: For many centuries the Catholic faithful (unopposed, in fact encouraged, by the magisterium) tenaciously adhered to their belief in Mary's glorious Assumption as forming part of their

[384] Cf. above, footnote 368.
[385] Cf. C. Piana, O.F.M., *Assumptio B. V. Mariae apud scriptores saeculi XIII* (Rome-Sibenic, 1942); id., *La morte e l'Assunzione della B. Vergine nella letteratura medievale*, in SM, 1 (Rome, 1948), 283–361; Balić, *Testimonia . . .* , 2 (Rome, 1950), an exhaustive collection of texts and pertinent literature from the time of the Council of Trent to the year 1950; M. Jugie, *op. cit.*, 360–500.

faith. Now, this universal and centuries-old belief could not have originated in a purely natural source (such as eye-witnesses, documentary evidence). Therefore, it must be traced back to divine revelation.

Was this revelation explicit or implicit? The very fact that we have no extant record of belief in the Assumption during the first three or four centuries is sufficient indication that this truth was not explicitly revealed by Christ to His Apostles and, through these, to the early Christians. Only in the hypothesis of an implicit revelation is it understandable why it took so many years before the faithful (under the guidance of the Holy Spirit and by a process of analysis and/or logical deduction) became more and more conscious of the fact that this doctrine was actually *implied* in other Marian truths taught by the Church.[386]

D. *The Sacred Liturgy.* Since the liturgy is the official prayer of the Church, and as such gives outward expression to Catholic belief, it has always been considered an index of paramount importance in establishing the existence of a given doctrine. In the specific case of the Assumption the argument from the liturgy has played a decisive role.

Historians are not in perfect agreement as to the exact time when the feast of the Assumption began to be celebrated in the Church.[387] The following information,

---

[386] Cf. E. M. Burke, C.S.P., *Doctrinal Development and the Assumption of Our Lady,* in AER, 116 (1947), 339–361.

[387] Cf. W. O'Shea, S.S., *The History of the Feast of the Assumption,* in *Thom,* 14 (1951), 118–132; C. Morin, S.S., *The Assumption in the*

briefly condensed, represents only the considered opinion
of some specialists in the field, and need not be accepted
as definitive.

(1) *In the East.* According to some, the most ancient
feast of the Assumption was observed in Syria in the
early 6th century.[388] At about the same time, there seems
to have existed a similar feast in the church of Alexandria
in Egypt.[389] As to Jerusalem, according to Capelle, the
earliest authentic reference to an observance of this
nature is furnished by St. Andrew of Crete (d. 740) at
the beginning of the 8th century.[390] An earlier feast entitled "The Day of Mary the Mother of God," kept on
August 15 from the second half of the 5th century, has
been considered by some scholars as the oldest celebration of the Assumption.[391] Others, on the contrary, claim
that the exclusive purpose of this early feast was to
honor Mary's divine Maternity recently defined (in 431)
at the Council of Ephesus.[392]

(2) *In the West.* It seems that Gaul was the first to
celebrate the feast in question (on January 18) at the

Liturgy, in SM, 4 (Montreal, 1948), 391–397; F. Antonelli, O.F.M.,
La festa dell'Assunzione nella liturgia romana, in SM, 1 (Rome, 1948),
225–239. Further literature in Carol, A *Bibliography of the Assumption,*
in *Thom,* 14 (1951), 133–160.

[388] Cf. B. Capelle, O.S.B., *L'Assunzione e la liturgia* (Rome, 1953),
19; V. González, O.S.B., *La dormición de María en las antiguas litur-
gias,* in EM, 9 (1950), 66.

[389] Capelle, *op. cit.,* 19; P. Gassó, O.S.B., *La Asunción en la liturgia;
sobre los orígenes de la fiesta,* in EM, 6 (1947), 140.

[390] Capelle, *op. cit.,* 14.

[391] Cf. Gordillo, *La muerte de María Madre de Dios en la tradición
de la Iglesia de Jerusalén,* in EM, 9 (1950), 60, 62; González, *art. cit.,*
66.

[392] Capelle, *op. cit.,* 8–9.

beginning of the 7th century,[393] as it appears from the Gothic Missal and other liturgical sources. Later on, owing to Roman influence, the date was transferred to August 15. In Rome itself, it was not until the second half of the 8th century that the liturgical commemoration of Mary's death, introduced by Pope Theodore I (642–649), became a distinct feast honoring the Assumption.[394] Nevertheless, even before this change of name took place, the Roman liturgy testified to a belief in Mary's prerogative. Thus we learn from the *Liber Pontificalis* that Pope St. Sergius I (687–701) decreed the famous collect *Veneranda* to be recited at the beginning of a solemn procession held in connection with the feast of the Dormition. This collect, which was in use until the 13th century, expressly mentions that, although Our Lady had died, yet she could not be held by the bonds of death.[395]

The liturgy, however, was not always uniformly assertive on our subject. For example, it was unfortunate that pseudo-Jerome's epistle *Cogitis me*, which showed great reserve in this matter, was actually incorporated into the office of the Assumption from the 10th century until the

---

393 Cf. A. Fayard, *L'Assomption: de la liturgie gallicane à la liturgie française*, in SM, 6 (Paris, 1950), 29–45; Gassó, *art. cit.*, 141–143.

394 Jugie, *op. cit.*, 195 favors the end of the 7th century; Gassó, *art. cit.*, 144, favors the middle of the same century; this view is shared by Antonelli, *art. cit.*, 232.

395 Cf. Capelle, *Mort et Assomption de la Vierge dans l'oraison "Veneranda,"* in EL, 66 (1952), 241–251; G. Brassó, O.S.B., *Contenido doctrinal de las fórmulas asuncionistas de la liturgia romana*, in EM, 6 (1947), 147–154.

reform of the breviary by Pope St. Pius V in 1568.[396] To be sure, this factor accounts largely for the disconcerting hesitations expressed in this connection by not a few writers in the Middle Ages.[396]

E. *Connection with other truths.* Mary's Assumption is not only in absolute harmony with other dogmas and accepted Catholic doctrines; it would seem to be even demanded by some of them.[397] In the bull of the definition Pius XII frequently stresses this phase of the dogma. Of particular importance in this connection are the divine Motherhood, the Immaculate Conception, and the Coredemption. The following is but an outline of the argument:

(1) *The Divine Motherhood.* Christ being an accomplished exemplar of perfect obedience to the law of God, He must have loved and honored His Mother in an exceedingly perfect manner, in accordance with the fourth commandment. Therefore, it is reasonable to be presumed that He wished to honor her by preserving her from the corruption of the grave and by granting to her an anticipated bodily glorification in heaven. This argu-

[396] Cf. E. Bourque, *Le sens de l'Assomption dans la liturgie,* in SM, 4 (1948), 169–174; Capelle, *op. cit.,* 28–39.

[397] Cf. K. J. Healy, O.Carm., *The Assumption among Mary's Privileges,* in *Thom,* 15 (1951), 72–92; E. M. Caggiano, O.F.M., *L'Assunzione della B. Virgine nei dommi mariani,* in SM, 1 (Rome, 1948), 617–644; J. Loosen, S.J., *Zusammenhang des Dogmas von der leiblichen Aufnahme Mariens in den Himmel mit den übrigen Mariengeheimnissen,* in *Die leibliche Himmelfahrt Mariens,* edited by the professors of St. Georgen, Frankfurt (Frankfurt, 1951), 71–81.

ment, while not apodictic in itself, is nevertheless one of great fittingness.[398]

(2) *The Immaculate Conception.* The argument has been authoritatively enunciated by Pius XII in the following words: "These two privileges (i.e., the Assumption and the Immaculate Conception) are most closely bound to one another. Indeed, Christ overcame sin and death by His own death; and the man who, through baptism, is supernaturally regenerated, has conquered sin and death through the same Christ. However, as a general rule, God does not wish to grant to the just the full effect of their victory over death until the end of time shall have come. And so it is that the bodies of even the just are corrupted after death, and that only on the last day will they be joined, each to his own glorified soul. Nevertheless, God has willed that the Blessed Virgin Mary should be exempted from this general law. By an entirely unique privilege she completely overcame sin through her Immaculate Conception, and therefore was not subject to that law of remaining in the corruption of the grave; nor did she have to wait until the end of time for the redemption of her body."[399]

(3) *The Coredemption.* As Coredemptrix, Our Blessed Lady was indissolubly associated with the Redeemer in His redemptive role and mission. Now, we

---

[398] Cf. G. Frénaud, O.S.B., *Preuve théologique de l'Assomption corporelle de Maria fondée sur le dogme de la maternité divine,* in BSFEM, 6 (1949), 121–147; Carol, *The Definability of Mary's Assumption,* in AER, 118 (March, 1948), esp. 167–168.

[399] AAS, 42 (1950), 754; Engl. ed., p. 6, nn. 4–5.

know from revelation that, in the case of Christ, the work of Redemption necessarily implied the utter destruction of Satan's dominion, one aspect of which is the state of permanent death until the end of time. Hence, we can scarcely assume that Our Blessed Lady was subject to this penalty for in this event she would be a victim of, rather than a victor over, the infernal foe. Mary's complete triumph, then, closely followed the pattern of Christ's triumph: like her own Son, she defeated death, not by not dying, but by not remaining dead.[400]

Corollary: On the Cult of Our Lady.

In view of the sublime prerogatives which Almighty God has so liberally bestowed on Our Blessed Lady, it is obvious that she is entitled to receive a distinct cult from all her children. This cult, which consists essentially in a grateful recognition of her unique dignity and exalted privileges, is technically called *hyperdulia,* and differs fundamentally from that of *latria* (worship given to God) and from that of *dulia* (veneration due to the saints).

The various elements which constitute our Marian cult are neatly summarized by Father Roschini as fol-

[400] Cf. Carol, *art. cit.,* in AER, 118 (March, 1948), 170–177; id, *De Coredemptione B. V. Mariae in quibusdam postulatis ad Sanctam Sedem delatis,* in MF, 48 (1948), 85–90; id., *The Apostolic Constitution "Munificentissimus Deus" and Our Blessed Lady's Coredemption,* in AER, 125 (October, 1951), 255–273; same article in *Mm,* 13 (1951), 237–256.

lows: "1) *Veneration*, by reason of the divine Maternity with regard to Christ; 2) *Love*, by reason of her spiritual Maternity with regard to all the mystical members of Christ; 3) *Gratitude*, by reason of her Coredemption or cooperation in the acquisition of all graces; 4) *Invocation*, by reason of her cooperation in the distribution of every single grace; 5) *Imitation*, by reason of her singular sanctity; 6) *Servitude*, by reason of her universal Queenship."[401]

The legitimacy of our Marian cult, whether directed to the person itself of Mary or to her relics or images, has been repeatedly and vigorously vindicated by the magisterium of the Church against the occasional attacks of non-Catholics. This is evident, for example, from the profession of faith incorporated in the bull of Pius IV (November 13, 1564),[402] from the decree of the Sacred Congregation of Rites (June 1, 1884),[403] and more recently from the encyclical *Mediator Dei* (November 20, 1947) of Pius XII.[404] The Bible itself offers some instances of special reverence given to the Mother of

---

[401] Roschini, *Summula Mariologiae* (Rome, 1952), 196–197.

[402] *DB*, 998. Cf. also *DB*, 986, and the decree of the Holy Office condemning the Jansenists' proposition: "Honor paid to Mary as Mary, is vain" (*DB*, 1316).

[403] *ASS*, 16 (1884), 526: "The Church honors the Queen and Sovereign of the Angels with a higher veneration above the other Saints; as Mother of God, she is entitled, not to an ordinary *dulia*, but to *hyperdulia*."

[404] Pius XII, *On the Sacred Liturgy*. Encyclical Letter *Mediator Dei* (New York, The America Press, 1948), 69, n. 169: "Among the Saints in heaven, the Blessed Virgin Mary, Mother of God, is venerated in a special way."

God. For example, the greeting of the Angel Gabriel, repeated later on by St. Elizabeth: "Blessed art thou among women" (Luke 1:28 and 42); to which we may add Our Lady's prophecy concerning herself: "Behold from henceforth all generations shall call me blessed" (Luke 1:48).

That a special Marian cult is not only legitimate, but also eminently suitable to further the glory of God, and most conducive to the practice of virtue among the faithful, is clearly implied in the traditional attitude of the Church relative to the establishment of Marian feasts, the encouragement of Marian devotions and the like. Here again the Sacred Liturgy, reflecting the official mind of the magisterium, furnishes pertinent testimonies in abundance.[405] Indeed, it is a commonly accepted view among Catholic authors that the cult of devotion to Our Lady (at least in some degree) is not only useful and profitable, but likewise hypothetically necessary for salvation. This position was recently corroborated by Pope Pius XII himself in his radio broadcast to the Marian Congress of Argentina (October 12, 1947) in which he stated that devotion to Mary "constitutes a fundamental element of Christian life, since we all need her assistance in the trials and dangers of the present life."[406]

As to the various manifestations of the Marian cult,

[405] Cf. Merkelbach, op. cit., 401; Pohle-Preuss, op. cit., 135–137.
[406] AAS, 39 (1947), 628.

such as feasts, prayers, devotions, sodalities and the like, their study would seem to fall rather under the heading of *historical* and *devotional* Mariology, and hence may be omitted in a dogmatic treatise such as ours.[407]

[407] Adequate information on these and related subjects may be found in E. Campana, *Maria nel culto cattolico,* 2nd ed., 2 vols. (Turin, 1944), and Roschini, *Mariologia,* 2nd ed., vol. 4 (Rome, 1948); also his more recent work *La Madonna secondo la fede e la teologia,* vol. 4 (Rome, 1954). The third volume of our *Mariology,* now in the course of publication by Bruce (Milwaukee), will be entirely devoted to the various phases of the Marian cult.

Index of Authors

SET UP, PRINTED AND BOUND BY BENZIGER BROTHERS, INC., NEW YORK